Beyond Feast
Or Famine

Daily Affirmations For
Compulsive Eaters

Susan K. Ward

Health Communications, Inc.
Deerfield Beach, Florida

Susan K. Ward
San Diego, California

© 1990 Susan K. Ward

ISBN 1-55874-076-7

Publisher: Health Communications, Inc.
              3201 S.W. 15th Street
              Deerfield Beach, FL 33442-8124

Cover design by Ana Bowen

DEDICATION

I dedicate this book to all of my clients who were so open and trusting in sharing their innermost thoughts.

I also dedicate this to my son Ryan for his continued support.

I owe a special thanks to G.L. Mohan for his exquisite sensitivity in editing these affirmations.

INTRODUCTION

These Daily Affirmations are for those of us who have problems with food — either because we eat too much or because we eat too little. Unlike those who have problems with drugs or alcohol, we cannot just cut food out of our lives but must learn to live in harmony with it and with the body that nature has given us. As we live day by day in our recovery we learn, with the help of these affirmations, to accept ourselves and our problems with food. In recovery we reach for the serenity of knowing that we do not have to measure up to others' expectations of weight, height or body type. In doing so we can free ourselves from the hold that food and eating have had over us.

Just as we live our lives day by day, so too we must spend time daily on our recovery. These Daily Affirmations are written to encourage each individual to follow their own path towards the many possibilities that are open to them. They have been written after years of experience working with those who have problems with compulsive eating in the hope that what has worked for them will also work for you.

Read an affirmation every day, preferably before breakfast, and learn to empower yourself to create a happy, fulfilling and balanced life. Discover that you are not alone as you deal with your issues day by day and one step at a time.

I begin today by affirming my self-worth. Each aspect of myself — physical, emotional and spiritual — needs to be acknowledged and nurtured. I eat the amount of food that satisfies me as I acknowledge my body's limits. I nurture my emotional needs by encouraging myself to express my feelings rather than control them by restricting food, overeating or binging. I take one step at a time during my recovery. I nurture my spiritual nature by acknowledging a Higher Power which gives me the strength to overcome any habitual behavior or thought. My conflict with food is a habit. I now take charge of changing my relationship with food.

* * *

Beginning today, I have all the strength and courage I need to make changes in my life.

The light within me opens me up to new life-promoting experiences. My openness allows me to trust myself. I relate to others with more openness as I risk becoming closer to the people I love. I release myself from the protection of food as I begin to face life with a new attitude. I no longer use food or a diet to keep me from attending or eating at social gatherings. I take small risks each day as I acknowledge my self-worth. I am willing to exchange my limited relationship with food for expanded relationships with myself and others.

*   *   *

I relate to others with more openness, using the light within to show the way.

Living and loving in the present helps me to be aware of my needs. It also helps me tune into the needs of others after my own are acknowledged and tended to. I am learning to give to myself and take care of myself in the same way I have given to others. I now use my past as my guide to the present. I acknowledge that I have needs and that I can ask others for help and nurturance. Life is more balanced now that I can give and accept nurturance for myself.

* * *

Living in the present helps me to express my needs and respond to the needs of others.

The power of my spirit to grow is the basis for my hope. The process of change continuing within me gives me faith in myself. I am now able to view all change as growth. I learn from my actions rather than allow my old behaviors to control me. I am willing to accept responsibility for all that I do because I am self-directed and motivated by my wants and needs. As I learn to recognize the true nature of my desires, I respect them and I am more able to respond to them to nurture myself.

*   *   *

I view all the changes taking place in my life as leading to growth and fulfillment.

I learn from my past. My hopes, my dreams, my struggles and my successes are my guiding lights. Today I look at myself as a complete person. I draw from all parts of my being to promote change and growth. I release myself from any guilt over the past as I acknowledge that my coping mechanisms were the best I had then. Binging or restricting food was a part of that way of life as I utilized all of my energy to survive. I am a survivor. Today I see life as a greater experience than survival; I am ready to ask much more of life. I am encouraging myself to reach beyond my former sense of the world and to become my best self.

*   *   *

Today I am encouraging myself to experience life fully, not merely to survive.

Looking to yet another new day, I am renewed by my strengthening sense of self-worth. I respect myself in a different way now. I acknowledge the value of my feelings and my personal expression. I respect the fragile nature of my newfound sense of self and challenge it only half as much as I think it can withstand. I allow my inner worth to grow in strength as I assure myself of its presence. My actions reflect this belief. I respect myself and ask for respect from others through my new sense of self. I am recovering.

* * *

Today I treasure my sense of self-worth and the quiet joy it brings me.

The warmth and glow of the sun is a reflection of the light within me and the peace it brings. I am allowing my inner harmony to guide my actions. I release myself from my conflict with food as I respond to my old emotional need for food during stressful times by refocusing my energy on my peaceful inner strength. I accept my former habit patterns as I challenge myself to find new healthy ways to soothe any anxiety I may have. My connection with the Higher Power reinforces my sense of harmony.

*   *   *

My inner harmony and spiritual tranquility are sources of strength I call upon to soothe me in times of stress.

Today I accept the challenge of being gentle with my body, treating it with the respect I deserve. In treating my body well, I reflect on my unique sensitivity. As I accept my vulnerability and my individuality, I acknowledge feelings I no longer wish to hide. I open myself to the personal expression that is uniquely mine. My sensitivity is an exquisite gift of nature. I accept this quality within me as I acknowledge my self-worth. I demonstrate this specialness by wearing something in my favorite color to remind me of my goal for today. I affirm myself each time I notice the color of my unique sensitivity.

*   *   *

Today I affirm myself by treating my body with gentleness and respect.

Today I view my struggle with food as a unique opportunity to learn about the intensity with which I want to live my life. My goal for today is to express myself openly, to the fullest sense of my self-worth. I no longer criticize myself for my conflict with food, but accept that I nurtured myself in the best way I knew at the time with the tools I was given. Now that I am aware of my behavior patterns, I gradually let go of the old means of coping and allow myself to explore new, healthy ways to meet my emotional needs. I accept my past as I learn better ways to nurture myself.

*   *   *

I use my conflict with food as an opportunity to explore and experience my life intensely.

I understand that breaking compulsive eating habits is a day-to-day process. Today I will begin with only one small aspect of my eating. Each small change is a building block that helps me reach my ultimate goal of being content with food. I am learning what the feeling of being satisfied is all about. I am accepting the gentle challenge of eating when I am hungry and stopping when I just feel full. I am learning to quiet my fears of not having enough with the constant reminder that food is always available to me. I know that I will not deprive myself of food since deprivation only sets me up for wanting more.

*   *   *

I am learning to quiet my fears of not having enough to eat. Food is always available to me.

I am learning to choose friends who appreciate my good qualities and support my efforts to win my struggle with food. The natural give-and-take of friendship is something I deserve to have in my life. It energizes me and gives me emotional nourishment that I greatly enjoy. On the other hand, I give myself permission to limit my contact with those people in my life who seem to judge me and who sabotage my efforts to discipline myself with food. I am better able now, with increased self-esteem, to support myself and elicit support for my expanding self-acceptance.

*   *   *

Today I choose as my true friends those who stand by me and accept my withdrawal from others who are not available to me.

My decisions today are based on my appreciation of myself and my needs as an individual. Being in the process of change, I am better able to understand my emotional needs and acknowledge their importance. I am now aware that in the past I ignored my own emotional needs and filled this void with food. I am also aware that I expected others to understand my needs when I was unable to identify them myself. Because blame and guilt no longer have any place in my new life as I become strong and self-reliant, I am more available to interact with others.

*   *   *

I am stronger each day and rejoice at being able to understand, express and meet my needs myself.

I am learning to nurture myself in the same way that I care for and nurture others. I am learning to recognize that I really want to be given to just as I give to others. As I learn to feed myself in a healthy way, I feel the self-respect and true caring this brings. Today I will do something special for myself that is not related to food, but which I will enjoy and which will make me aware of my specialness.

*   *   *

As I let go of my old destructive ways, I am gradually filling my life with self-caring and actions that signify my growth within.

I begin today in the spirit of self-renewal. As I let go of the past and live in the present moment, I am aware that I can renew my spirit and the sense of my worth throughout the day. My new resolve to change gets stronger as each day goes by. I am aware that there can be small setbacks along the way, but this new sense of renewal assists me in letting them go without disturbing me. I am living in the present with self-acceptance, never losing the vision of my long-term goal.

*   *   *

I begin and end each day with a strong sense of resolve and a renewed commitment to my own evolving process of change.

I find that being free to express myself, I have the support of my inner strength that manifests itself as needed. I am learning that I am never given more difficulty than I can handle, for I have surmounted every hurdle in my resolve to free myself from my addiction. Each step along the way, I am finding new and different means by which I can tap my strength without giving it away, always keeping a healthy reserve for re-newal and growth. I am now aware that I have used eating to compensate for my other needs. Letting go of food allows me to appreciate my sense of self and encourages me to be my own best friend.

*   *   *

I am learning to tap my strength in difficult moments and gaining a fine appreciation of my inner spirit.

The courage to change comes from within me. I believe in myself. I am learning to trust myself and to accept my humanness, with all of the qualities of imperfection that go along with it. I am learning to view myself in the spirit of becoming, becoming all that I can be. The Higher Power has entrusted me with a unique set of abilities which I am learning to expand to the fullest. Fear has no place in my process of growth except as a stumbling block to be overcome. Living my life creatively, I am beginning to love and understand myself and others.

*   *   *

I renew my courage each time I let an old pattern go and transform it into a positive new pattern of behavior.

Love comes in many forms. My new way of loving and respecting myself is to listen to my body cues — to eat when I am hungry, to drink when I am thirsty and to stop when I am satisfied. Accepting my body's natural signals for nourishment renews my spirit and increases my self-worth. The child within me, so long ignored, rejoices at being heard and acknowledged. My body is becoming my friend. Removing my conflict with food gives me more energy to truly live my life. I participate in and contribute to life as I listen to my body's cues.

* * *

I am giving myself permission, a little at a time, to explore my body's responses to the natural order of life.

I understand that motivation is a step-by-step process. Progress is made with each little change I make and with each day I decide to begin anew. I am gaining an understanding of the true meaning of small changes, the subtleties of the responses that are first occurring within me and the tiny transformations that are taking root. They manifest themselves outwardly only when they are ready to be seen. Each time the process of change — denial, depression, anger and acceptance — takes place more quickly, it brings positive and sure results.

*   *   *

I cherish the subtle signs of growth I see in myself and feel the excitement that comes with the germination of rebirth.

Today is the beginning of a new habit, not just the breaking of an old one. Today I focus on my new approach to food and, therefore, to life as a whole. I will focus on the energy I have when I eat only to satisfy physical hunger rather than as a way to soothe emotional needs. I nourish my body by eating foods that will build my inner strength. I nourish my mind by exploring different subject areas that are rewarding to my sense of self. I relinquish my habit of spending time unnecessarily on calorie counting and continuous thinking about food, so that I may renew my natural interest in other subjects. I nourish my spirit by acknowledging my relationship with the Higher Power.

*   *   *

I am learning to be satiated and to take in the world with my other senses of touching, hearing, seeing and smelling.

I overcome inertia when I take a step, any step forward. Each step is a movement forward and the momentum of the movement subtly takes over, leading me to con-.tinuous change and growth. By being open to change and growth and guidance from those that I can trust, I overcome any reticence that I have to venture into uncharted territory. I now embrace the small steps I am comfortable taking, knowing that with each success I am ready for yet bigger steps that lead to my health and success. As the breath replenishes the body, my movement forward replenishes the spirit of renewal.

*   *   *

I am open and ready to conquer new challenges that are presented to me today.

I deserve to be satisfied with my body. I cleanse my attitudes, values and beliefs towards my body. I allow positive attitudes to replace negative ones. I create a vision of the body I wish to have, based on my natural body rather than looking outside myself for an idea which I may not be able to achieve. I allow my goals to be realistic and my faith in myself to be firm and steady. I am my own best friend and am grateful for my ability to give myself the support I need. I accept my body and appreciate its functional aspect as well as its aesthetic aspect. I confirm my belief in myself by consolidating my positive experiences in accepting my body image.

*   *   *

I move closer to contentment with my natural attributes as I appreciate my body aesthetically.

I am taking full responsibility for the conditions in my life. I am aware that I am a unique individual who can choose to change a situation or have it remain as it is. The energy of the universe and the guidance of the Higher Power who created me are available to me in making my choice. I have the energy within me to design my life. As long as I focus on others as the problem or the solution, I understand that I choose to remain as I am. In order to elicit my own power to change, I am learning to focus on my feelings, my ideas and my consciously chosen actions.

* * *

My goal is to accept myself. Only then can I actively make changes if I choose to do so.

As I release the fear of owning my personal power, I am able to gain awareness in my natural abilities. I feel my strength coming from within me and radiating outward. At first I am only able to glimpse the beginning of my center. The more I concentrate on focusing on my own inner core of strength, the closer I get to the healing images that will sustain me in my recovery. The more comfortable I am with myself, the more I can accept my abilities and tap the energy I need to fulfill my potential. Loving myself is the key to remaining in tune with my abilities. I possess all that I need to grow.

*   *   *

I am gradually accepting that I am neither too much nor too little with regard to my natural abilities.

I am establishing a healthy balance in my life between my wants and needs. I am able to acknowledge my desire to be close to someone without being overwhelmed. I am feeling love for myself and others and I can express it in a way that conveys what I desire — a healthy mutuality based on love and respect. I am free to grow just as I encourage others to grow. I am responsible only for my own actions.

*   *   *

I can support and love others but I can only take responsibility for myself.

I am responsible for how I interact with others and how I allow others to interact with me. I am not a victim of situations or events because I am taking a responsible approach to my life. I am learning from my past mistakes in relating to people and look to the future as an opportunity to refine the interpersonal skills I am learning today. I am alive and present in each interaction so that I may act with my whole being rather than as an observer. I ask of others no more than what I am willing to give in each situation. I am respectful of myself and therefore I am respectful of others.

*   *   *

As I creatively interact with the world, I take every opportunity to assert myself as an opportunity for change.

25

As I become more honest with and re-spectful towards myself, I can be more honest and respectful towards other people. My inner light is guiding me and my self-respect is no longer based on the approval of others. I can accept their approval as support; however, my own standards are what I am learning to live by. I am receptive to compliments because I am worthy of my own respect and approval. I am not perfect and therefore I do not expect others to be perfect either.

*   *   *

In doing my best, I continue to grow in my self-respect, without depending on the approval of others.

To develop my personal power is to let go of built-up anger, anxiety and resentment. It gives me the courage to open up to the world and develop a creative force that allows me to interact freely without fear. As I choose to express myself, I reinforce my sense of self-worth and personal conviction. I am able to overcome feelings of helplessness and fear by affirming my inner sense of self-acceptance and making a positive statement in the external world.

* * *

Today I look for the opportunities to convey my sense of worth and purpose to those around me.

I now act in the world rather than react. Reacting to others keeps me in self-denial. Initiating actions is moving forward. It furthers my goal of autonomy and independence. I no longer need food to keep me from asserting myself. I am able to set my own limits, make free choices and relinquish feelings of guilt in my self-assertiveness. This allows me the freedom to be myself in each situation since I am not trying to be all things to all people. I do not push myself to perform for others, but rather take pleasure and pride in my accomplishments. I am pleased with my newfound ability to assert myself.

*   *   *

I assert myself by acknowledging my uniqueness and choosing to act rather than react.

Food is no longer an answer to my internal struggles. It cannot provide the love and caring I can give myself and graciously accept from others. Food satisfies my bodily hunger. Love and self-acceptance satisfy my emotional needs. I am providing nurturance for myself. I choose the company of supportive people and I allow myself the right to refuse company when I need to nurture myself by being alone. I trust the plan of the Higher Power for me and find peace and contentment within myself.

*   *   *

Food no longer resolves my problems. It remains enjoyable, but is only one of many rewards I receive at all levels of life.

I understand now that I have the freedom
to explore and create my own reality. Each
day I become more aware of my body and its
needs. I am in tune with my natural processes and understand that by allowing my
body to determine when I will eat, I am
freeing my mind of preconceived notions
regarding food. Food is nourishment. I nourish myself when I am hungry. I can eat to
the point of satisfaction and stop before I
get too full. This is a new and exciting discovery for me. I am learning that food will
always be a part of my life. I am choosing
to place it in its proper place in my multifaceted life.

*   *   *

Food is for the healthy functioning of my body.
I am now free to experiment with other means of
nurturing myself.

I am learning to be myself without apology and without the need for someone else's approval. I am my own loving reflection of my vision for myself. I keep the healthy image of my body alive as I envision my best realistic body. I release my hold on a fantasy figure, an ideal which I cannot achieve without extreme methods of manipulating my food intake. I reach deep within my spirit to arrive at the best possible solution to each problem, knowing that I am doing what I can. I place my emphasis on emotional, physical and spiritual health and well-being. Each aspect of my growth gets nurturing attention from me each and every day.

*   *   *

As I accept each aspect of myself and have faith in the power of my own healthy renewal, I take pride in who I am and who I am becoming.

I am realizing my potential by my willingness to defend my human rights. I can say no to the world with my voice rather than with food. My expression of my values and beliefs reinforces my self-worth. While in the past food served as a substitute for self-expression, now my words and actions affirm me. I command self-respect and as I increase my awareness of myself, I am able to further my goals and my purpose in life. As my belief system changes, so does my outward appearance. I am beginning to love my body and the results show gradually. Knowing that I am changing my attitude to life continues to motivate me to experiment with my self-expression.

* * *

In boldly expressing my values and beliefs, I am reinforcing my self-worth.

I feel a healthy sense of mutuality and sharing with my family and friends. Joining with others renews my sense of purpose and meaning. Others value my presence and my contribution to their lives. I am worthy of all the love that naturally comes to me in this way. I respect myself and the love I generate. The more open and honest I am with myself and my recovery, the more open and honest I can be with others. What I am able to give to myself, I notice I can receive from others also.

*   *   *

I am discovering the fulfillment that comes from sharing myself with others.

I am setting a realistic and attainable goal for myself today. I no longer set my goals so high that I meet with failure. In doing so, I establish a pattern of success for myself. I am able to meet the expectations that I have of myself. I am learning to accept myself as I am and understand that I can only transform those qualities I recognize and acknowledge in myself. I cannot change what I cannot accept. Acceptance precedes change. Life is a series of small changes that build up into even bigger successes.

*   *   *

I set myself realistic and attainable standards to support my changes.

I focus on a positive aspect of my body that I like, one that seems to be reassuring to my self-esteem. As I am able to center my attention on this positive aspect, I give it a name which signifies a quality I have in myself. I continue to act to strengthen the positive aspects of my body and my personality. This focus is the foundation upon which I am able to build other positive qualities. In my mind's eye I see a picture of my best body. I recognize myself in it with pleasure.

*   *   *

I center my attention on the positive, I am a powerful focus of life and energy.

I deserve to be successful in my life. Today I begin with remembering and acknowledging the successes I have achieved thus far in my life. I will continue to develop myself and strive for further success each day. Achieving success is something always within my reach, for it can be small as well as large. Each success is fertile ground for reaping future successes. I am learning to trust the neglected part of myself that encourages and supports my growth. I can have all that I want and will continue to be successful.

* * *

I am in charge of my personal fulfillment and allow my inner light to lead me to success.

I know that I can embrace my new, healthy behaviors with vigor, just as I have held on to my old patterns with such tenacity. These new patterns of eating and relating to my body are gradually replacing the old ways that were so destructive to my self-esteem. Even though I am aware that the old ways of thinking and acting were comfortable, I realize that the new patterns are for my benefit. I honor and respect my cycle of growth and change. Today I make a list of the behaviors I have already changed and I congratulate myself for my efforts. I also make a list of new goals and I choose one to focus on this day.

*   *   *

My new healing ways are slowly becoming my entire way of life.

As I review my past, I visualize the time when food was no longer a comfort to me but a compulsion, with preconceived rules and guidelines. It became a time more of pain than of comfort. And since I always changed the rules about eating, it became an added source of frustration; my solution then became a problem. Looking back and knowing what I know now, I am able to find new healthy ways to comfort myself. Now I understand how I allowed food to control my life and forgive myself for having been unable to predict the future.

* * *

By recalling my past, I am choosing to live in the present with faith in myself and the Higher Power that guides me.

I willingly risk loving my body and accepting myself. I no longer deprive myself of food nor do I overindulge my body with it. In the process of recovering from compulsive eating and compulsive dieting, I am gradually coming to understand and acknowledge the feelings of loving my body. I respect myself and accept the risk of feeling the natural signals of hunger and fullness. Knowing that this takes time comforts me. It does not make me pressure myself to master the process, but gives me the space to relax into it.

*   *   *

I am giving myself the luxury of reawakening my awareness of my body signals and nurturing my inner spirit.

The dawn of a new day breathes new life into my commitment to nourish my body, mind and spirit. Each day I pratice one new habit. As the positive behaviors increase my confidence in the process of my becoming whole, I am able to see my growth and feel the strength of my commitment to myself. The respect I grant myself and my process affects my relationships with other people in a positive manner. The more open and accepting I am with myself, the more open and trusting I am with others.

*   *   *

Today I stand committed to nourish myself, my habits and my relationships to empower me on the course of wholeness.

Love flows in an easy exchange between me and my family, my friends and all others I meet. My loving acceptance of myself glows through me. I am continually affirming myself daily and validating my own feelings in the process of recovery. I am learning to ask others for what I want, not relying on food to meet my emotional needs. The void that I had hoped food would fill, I am now filling with love, trust, self-esteem and self-confidence. I am gaining confidence in my body and in my unique abilities as a contributing member of society.

*   *   *

Loving acceptance of myself is the key to a new life of self-confidence and contentment.

Releasing my judgments about myself helps me to stop judging and criticizing others. The new nurturing ways in which I treat myself foster my attitude of acceptance towards others. I am learning to re-create my image of myself by replacing an old negative thought with a realistic positive one. My dreams for myself are becoming a reality, gradually unfolding before my eyes. With mind focused on a tangible goal, I am able to endure the small setbacks in the process of changing my old attitudes, values and beliefs. I recognize that the old ways of thinking about myself and others promote a static existence with little surprises and little joy.

*   *   *

As a butterfly sheds its unnecessary cocoon, so do I release myself from the old layers into discovering the fullness of my natural being.

My hopes, my dreams, my struggles and my successes are my guiding lights. Life is a process of growth and regression. While I seem to make progress, I also realize that I seem to slip back into old habits. I am being gentle with myself at this time, treating myself as I would a child who slipped and fell. I value the child within me who longs for my support and kindness. I am learning that gentleness reaps its own rewards. As the light of renewal shines through me and I am aware of the Higher Power within me, I renew my faith in my spirit and in my human qualities.

*   *   *

I am my own support when I stumble. I am gratified to see that each time I slip back, it takes less time to recover.

Living and loving in the present allows me to be more spontaneous and more aware of my true needs. Continuing to grow in self-awareness fosters self-acceptance and releases me from the conflict I have with food. I understand that I was asking of food something only self-acceptance can provide. The power of my spirit to grow is based on the limitless potential that my self-esteem engenders. My process of change leads me to have faith in myself.

*   *   *

I can tune into myself and be aware of my body and my feelings at any time.

44

I am dedicating my energies to the conscious choice between enjoying the nourishing foods I choose for my body and nourishing my emotions. I am able to choose another way of acknowledging my feelings as I accept that food does not meet my emotional needs but creates other problems for me. I am now able to release the judgments I had about myself in the past because it was the only way I knew to respond to my needs then. I am proud of my new way of approaching feelings and food. In loving myself, I am able to let go of the fear of being without comfort in other areas of my life.

*   *   *

By separating the issues of feelings and food, I become completely at ease with myself.

I am my positive thoughts. I carry into this day and this life the fulfillment of who I am. Love, life and my laughter are the vibrations that keep me moving along life's way. The formative process of change I am undergoing is my new way of parenting myself and creating the person I am becoming. My pulse quickens when I feel myself fulfilling my aspirations. The excitement of it leads me to affirm the true change that occurs with each new affirming message that I acknowledge.

*   *   *

I am my own positive thoughts.

Allowing growth to occur calls forth my strength, my sense of balance and my willingness to take risks. Risking in areas of trust and mutuality with others allows me to enjoy my own presence as well as the presence of others. Letting go of my struggle with food frees me to spend productive energy on my growth. Dieting, binging and purging reduce the physical and emotional energy available to me and others in my life. I acknowledge my right to eat and to enjoy food. My life is in order when food has its natural place in it. I utilize my newfound ability to support my growth by taking the time to consider what I am asking food to do for me when I feel the urge to binge or restrict.

*   *   *

I give myself the gift of food for my physical well-being and nurturance.

Learning to trust means first trusting my Higher Self, the wisdom of my own body and the depth of my commitment to change. In the past, I was always willing to look to others for solutions to problems in my life. Deep within, I know now that the change has to first come from me. Today I am beginning to exercise the decision with love and respect for myself. My choosing to change myself comes from an openness to explore my options, not from a position of resistance. I do this for myself, not going against anyone else.

*   *   *

Today I am determined to act out of true love for myself and with my health in mind.

Today I reflect on the child within me who continues to feel needy and wants to eat past the point of fullness. I choose today to begin feeding the child what he or she wants but protect him or her from eating too much. I am teaching this little person to respect hunger cues by eating a small amount of food that is truly satisfying. I think about the quality of the experience rather than the quantity of food I eat. Slowly, gradually, I am re-educating my body to perceive the internal cues which tell me that I am hungry. As with any child whom I love, I am aware growth involves time, moving forward and slipping back. This is the nature of change and I welcome its arrival.

* * *

I am focusing on the process of being a new parent to the child within.

I am changing my life's patterns. While that may not always be evident to me in a visible form, I keep my vision of my goal continuously alive, building a positive foundation for growth by affirming myself every day. I am forward-looking and ever aware of choosing what is in my best interest and in the best interest of those I love. I release the hold on the past since I know that thinking about it only keeps it alive in my mind. I let it go so that I may be present in my life today. I actively live my life today to make it the best day it can be. This new opportunity to change my life is my second chance for living my life creatively.

*　　*　　*

I am keeping my vision of my goal continuously alive.

I am in control of what I choose to give and what I choose to receive. This is an assertive statement I can make in my life. I can now choose to give to myself and to others; therefore, I no longer have to resist saying no. When I give from a spirit of love and sharing, I am able to let go of any connection to the gift, whether it be a gift of time or a gift that is tangible. I am joyous in my approach towards life and appreciate the healthy give and take in relationships. I make it a practice to give myself something small each day so that I do not resort to food as a way of meeting unmet needs.

*   *   *

My ability to choose gives me the freedom to receive and the freedom to give.

I am aware that breaking the habit of compulsive eating requires devotion to discipline and awareness of my physical and emotional needs. I am learning that discipline is different from control, for control implies deprivation and scarcity while discipline implies choosing discreetly in the midst of abundance. Choosing what I want to eat is a freeing act. I do not have to overeat or restrict food because I now have what I need and want to nourish myself. As I nourish myself on a physical and an emotional level, I am the parent to my process of change.

*   *   *

Today I free myself by choosing what I need instead of giving into compulsion.

I am continually capable of growing and learning. I am a witness to this fact as I reflect on the patterns of my life. In areas in which I have stopped growing, I choose a different path in order to effect change. Looking back, I understand that eating was a way to alleviate painful feelings; my need for food was a misplaced need for true comfort and solace. As I release myself from the past, I am able to choose more effective ways to express my feelings. In doing so, I experience a sense of freedom that food was not able to offer. I rejoice in my spirit of renewal.

*   *   *

I amaze myself with my ability to effect beneficial changes.

Loving myself empowers me to extend myself to others. Being truly in possession of my loving self, I heighten my ability to share. I take time to care for my own needs by listening to myself. I drink when I am thirsty, sleep when I am sleepy, eat when I am hungry and ask for attention from others when I need companionship. As I satisfy my basic needs, I am able to acknowledge my higher level of needs and wants. As I acknowledge myself and share myself, my abundance truly grows.

*   *   *

Today I take time to listen to myself and to ask for inner guidance.

In reviewing the choices I have made in my life, I acknowledge that I did the best I could with the knowledge I had at my disposal. I am not trying to change the past but only look to the possibilities in the present. With the confidence that I can change, I am encouraging myself to let go of the past and move fully into the present. I am inspired with the courage to create my life as an artist paints a canvas. I use the tools from the past, choosing those that I discern have benefited me. I have the courage to shape my life anew. I recreate it lovingly for myself and for those in my life. I seek help from the Higher Power in accepting responsibility for my choices.

*   *   *

Today I remind myself of the opportunities for growth that are here before me.

I look at my body as a work of art and the accumulation of all the experiences in my life, both positive and negative. I acknowledge its vulnerability and strength, which is my human legacy. My body has been useful in protecting me. It has used the information which I have given it and the inherent physiological knowledge that has been passed from generation to generation. I respect it as I respect my best friend. In doing this, I increase the love that I have for myself as a whole person.

*   *   *

From this time on, I will be grateful to my body and respect it as my friend.

56

Embracing the inherent birthright of my sex, I accept all aspects of my collective similarity and the expression of the uniqueness that lies within me. I embrace each opportunity to renew my commitment to my further development. My body, mind and spirit are joining together in a new way to enrich my experience. I temper my quest for a healthy way to live my life with a respect for my past and the choices I have made. I fulfill myself as a whole person as I accept my sexuality and the challenges which I choose to meet in this life. Letting go of my dependence on food and looking at each aspect of my life opens me up to new ways of relating to the world.

*   *   *

I accept my femininity/masculinity as I manifest myself in my body.

I am learning to feel my emotions more intensely rather than withdraw numbly into food and isolation. I gladly release the guilt I have harbored about my eating in the past; I accept what I have learned about myself. I nurture myself with the emotional richness of my process. As I witness the cycles in nature, I recognize my own cycles as part of the whole. Expanding my range of feelings has allowed me to make new choices for my life and to release myself from the patterns of yesterday. My efforts to learn about life give me the energy and encouragement to continue to look for yet newer solutions.

*   *   *

I experience my emotional intensity as an ability to feel with exquisite sensitivity.

As I move into the light, it illuminates my own vision of the end to my compulsive eating. I picture my body in its *ideal form*, the form that is most recognizably my true self. I am realistic with my goals for my body and allow it to adjust naturally to a healthy size and weight. I am the best that I can be today and I have faith in my ability to sustain my emotional and physical well-being in the future. The light within guides me into the present state of harmony in which I accept changes and welcome tomorrow.

*   *   *

I have confidence in myself to continue developing my physical, emotional and spiritual life.

My emphasis is on living my life in the present. Living in the present allows me to witness nature on a new level. It allows me to experience the memory of my past and to see it as a part of the whole. Living in the present encourages me to eat only when I am hungry and to feel truly satisfied. I am alive and spontaneous in the present. I love myself and those around me. I am free to express my feelings and my thoughts. I can give and expect nothing in return. I am able to let go of preconceived ideas about how life *should* be and am able to explore the present as all that there is. This way of life is very freeing and exhilarating for me.

*   *   *

I live my life for today as I gain the proper perspective on myself.

My sense of timing, my clarity and my flexibility in communicating with others are assets to me. I am free to allow full expression to all my emotions, knowing that my self-esteem is strengthened with each communication. I allow others the same degree of freedom I give myself. The more I guide myself to fulfill my potential, the more I am able to foster growth and healthy independence in others. I am especially sensitive to the needs of others. I now give freely of myself and have faith that the joy of giving is my reward. I notice that my need to eat because of unfulfilled relationships diminishes as my relationship with myself is clear and harmonious.

*   *   *

I communicate what I need and am honest in all my communications.

I know when situations are to my benefit
by trusting my intuition and giving credence
to my belief system. My inner light shines
through me, for what I believe and experience internally is expressed in my outer
countenance. I have a magnetic quality
which draws others to me. I am open in a
positive, enlightening manner and have released my needs to depend on others. I rely
on myself and am interdependent in a
healthy, fruitful way. What attracts me to
others is the joy of interacting on a spiritual
and emotional level that fosters mutual respect and growth.

*   *   *

*I accept my special qualities with humility and
know that this is a gift.*

My sense of emotional well-being and contentment is a source of my ever increasing strength and inner peace. I am able to live my life to the fullest, now that I experience enthusiasm and vitality from my inner being. Positive thoughts breed positive energy throughout my being and in my interactions with others. Today I reflect on my positive qualities and acknowledge them with joy. Any negative thoughts that come into my consciousness are released through a window I create in my mind. My strength to resist their influence over me is increased each time I reflect on my recovery and my joy in life.

* * *

Contentment, which comes to me naturally today, is the source of my strength, enthusiasm and positive outlook.

As my healing process continues, I reinforce the self-generating power that is the basis of my healthy functioning. I respect and honor my emotional, physical and spiritual needs, knowing that denial and overindulgence are but two sides of the same coin. I can eat with pleasure and experience fulfillment from the inside out. My healthy, respectful eating habits satisfy me without depriving me of the taste and texture of the foods I enjoy. Recognizing this on a daily basis through my daily affirmations and positive visualizations assists my growth and provides the bountiful gifts that are justly mine to receive. I enjoy an overflowing abundance in many areas of my life.

*   *   *

Today I renew and regenerate my faith in the power within me that helps me to grow in the ebb and flow of life.

I sense the need for restraint for the benefit of my body's health and the need to let go for my emotional health. I experience the balancing of control and release from the center of my being, from the same center in which I experience joy and peace and fulfillment. I accept the dynamic principle of harmony on a physical, emotional and universal level. If I withhold food too tightly, then my body becomes anxious to release itself from hunger. Restraining my emotions works in the same fashion. I now know how to give credence to my needs and desires and can balance the sensuality of pleasure with the self-respect of discipline. In learning to be truly satisfied, I feel fulfilled.

*   *   *

As I experience control and release in a balanced manner, I am free of the burden of extremes.

I am awed at my power of renewal and
recovery. My ability to heal myself is a source
of joy for me. I embrace the opportunity to
participate fully in giving to the child within
me so that I can meet the needs of my more
impulsive self and satisfy a deep need within
me to receive nurturance. I enjoy receiving
on a physical, emotional and spiritual level. I
feel grounded and fulfilled in my efforts to
receive pleasure and satisfaction. I trust that
my needs will be met now that I am able to
recognize the cry of the child within me. I
accept the necessity of satisfying that particular part of my personality so that I may
grow on other levels. I put the building blocks
of my personality in the appropriate places,
knowing that my personal development will
follow in an orderly fashion.

*   *   *

*Satiating the inner child's hunger for attention
allows me to nourish the strength of my ego.*

I am truly free to utilize my creative powers to define and enhance my life. Being alive and responsive to the energies around me and within me, I am able to share my life generously. When I share my abundance with others, I am able to establish a healthy balance between what I give others and what I give myself. I no longer expect from the act of giving to receive love and approval in return. There is freedom now in my giving. I let go of my attachment to my gift so that I may move on to other tasks at hand. As I enjoy life's abundance and humbly accept the privileges I have received, life's riches are mine for the asking.

*   *   *

The abundance in my life is evidence of my ability to give to myself and others.

I utilize my natural abilities to solve any difficulty I face today. I reach deep within my spirit to arrive at the best possible solution to each stumbling block, knowing that I am doing what I can at this point in time. I see that I have always done this, whether or not I now agree with the solutions of yesterday. I fully understand the role food played in my life and empathize with the child within me who resorted to that solution for comfort in a time of pain. This little person continues to require support in transition from the use of food to the expression of the true self. Only by expressing my feelings will I release myself from the child's dependency on food. Releasing food's power over me gives me the freedom I deserve.

*   *   *

I am gradually releasing myself from the bindings of the past.

I am restoring the natural balance of my inner and outer life. My outer actions, expressions and my body reflect my true self, my inner world. As I feel comfortable with myself, I know that I am ready for others to share in my beauty. Being able to release the need for performing and conforming to get the approval of others helps me to integrate my body, mind and spirit. My struggles and conflicts have been considerably lessened since this discovery. My only challenge is to live in the present and to learn to appreciate what I am feeling on a minute-by-minute basis. As I release the child within me, I can see and appreciate the expression of the child within others, including those in my care.

* * *

I create my own life and channel my energies in directions that will benefit me and others.

Being a friend to myself allows me to be a friend to others. People have been placed in my world to assist me in creating myself. No one is above me or below me; we are all created equal. The more I can appreciate myself, the more I can appreciate others. As I learn to commune with nature, I learn to commune with myself on a deep spiritual level. I acknowledge the depth of my feeling and my sensitivity towards my environment. By participating to the fullest, I can derive the maximum benefit in my life. Following both the natural rhythm of life and my own natural rhythm allows me to be a participant in life rather than a spectator.

*　　*　　*

I was created to be active and alive; I am fulfilling my potential.

I am willing to risk the disapproval of others in order to state my true feelings in a healthy, assertive way. My awareness of my feelings is the first step that releases them from being hidden away as secrets. I am able to do this because I believe in myself and the inherent strength I possess. While striving to know my real feelings, I separate those I see as merely acceptable and compliant. I may continue to choose to act upon what I see as "the right thing to do" until I become comfortable with positive self-expression. When I believe that holding them back will be harmful to my growth process, I express my feelings. I have the courage to trust that this process is my new guide in the journey of life.

*   *   *

I no longer hide my feelings, for being honest and true to myself is my primary goal.

71

Where previously there was safety in pleasing others, now there is safety and strength in pleasing myself and expressing my true feelings. Through trial and error I experience my true feelings and acknowledge my real needs. The love I offer myself is unconditional acceptance. It is my humanity I am accepting. Any feeling I experience is valid. I am young in this process of discovery and give myself the license to err. What a relief to release myself from the perfectionism and conditional acceptance that has heretofore been a habit! I acknowledge that my eating was connected with these stringent demands placed on me very early in life.

* * *

As I accept myself body, mind and spirit, I give myself the freedom and space I need for transformation.

Letting go of the old patterns allows me to experience the pain and discomfort I have been attempting to hide for many years. I am mourning the loss of an old self and accepting the fact that I reacted to my environment rather than having acted from true feelings. I was externally motivated — I acted for other people. Their happiness was more important to me than my own. Changing my focus from others to my own attitudes, values and beliefs is a lengthy process. Denial, sadness, anger and depression are natural feelings at this time. I allow myself to experience them. I trust myself to go through this process and arrive at the peace, contentment and harmony that I know are mine for the asking.

* * *

Each day as I let go and reaffirm myself, I become stronger.

I am regaining my equilibrium. The aura of confidence and success that I radiate reflects my positive experience of the changes in myself. I am a person of substance and distinction and my newfound ability to accept my positive qualities allows me to express these attributes in all my actions. I accept with humility and responsibility the gifts I have been given. My duty is to develop my positive characteristics to the fullest. I accept this challenge and continue to explore my excellence. I cease my demand for perfection as I accept myself as a whole person. Whatever has been given to me in the way of gifts and abilities or privileges, I now feel comfortable sharing with others as I manifest myself to the fullest.

*   *   *

I can show the world what I really am without demanding too much of myself or attempting to hide my true self.

In any recovery process, I am aware that there are relapses or setbacks in which I will revert to old ways of thinking. I think of any relapse as temporary and give myself permission to revisit patterns of yesterday. I am easy with myself and understand my humanity. Because eating has been my friend for so long, I know that at times it may be the first thing I turn to in times of stress. As time goes on and positive behavior replaces the old maladaptive behavior, the backsliding will decrease. As for today, it is another positive day in the healing process. I know that I am improving by the length of time between relapses and by the speed with which I move through them.

*   *   *

I know that I am in the process of letting go and I accept this part of change.

My love for myself demonstrates my ability to affirm myself. I affirm my own happiness, my own growth and my own freedom. The love I have for myself is patient and kind. It is unconditional love based on a true regard for my whole being — body, mind and soul. This manner of loving myself is the opposite of selfishness. Unconditional acceptance is satisfying, whereas selfishness, synonymous with greed which creates anxiety, never satiates. In this gentle self-love, I am able to see myself in a new light. It illuminates me with an emphasis on my positive qualities and with my ability to accept aspects of myself I previously chose to ignore. It is a beacon of light in the turmoil of recovery.

*   *   *

My love for myself is the basis of my ability to love another.

My mastery over compulsive eating increases my strength and my fervor to be the best I can be. The possibilities are limitless! I am open to spontaneity and to interacting with others openly and honestly. I am getting to know my body and trust its ability to give me signals and feedback regarding hunger and feelings. I now know the meaning of intuition and the power of acting on my own instinctive knowledge that has always been with me. Unveiling the layers of my insight into myself continues to be a fascinating process. I love myself!

*   *   *

I can trust myself.

Open-mindedness leads to new growth and new opportunities. As I review my life, I am able to see that I am at my happiest when I am open to new ideas and novel ways of seeing things. My life takes another fork in the road and I congratulate myself on being able to take risks with good judgment and faith in myself. It works for me because I support myself with an eye on my growth in the future. Being the best I can be is my goal for today and for ever.

* * *

At this turning point in my life, I open myself to new ways of growth.

I am comforted by the risks I am beginning to take with my body. This new direction gives me a sense of wholeness and completion. I am trying new physical activities since I can now accept my body's processes as being a fundamental part of this integrative process of growth. This new awareness of my body helps me to accept those parts of myself I have denied for so long. Regular exercises and creative expression free me from prior patterns and allow me to explore the world on a new sensory level. I am amazed by the profound impact of simple body movements and the integration and peace which they bring.

* * *

Today I enjoy the renewed vigor I experience when I try new physical activities.

I am aware that when I exhibit aggressive behavior, I am covering up the fear and weakness I am feeling at that moment. I know that the consequences of my aggressive behavior will inevitably reinforce my feelings of inferiority, loss of control and alienation from others. I now know that my compulsive eating, restricting or purging are actually these aggressive behaviors turned towards myself. It follows, then, that my alienation from myself will follow as well as increased fear of my own impulses and lack of safety in my body. Learning to trust my body is a key component in eliminating this behavior. I release my self-imposed alienation by acknowledging myself and accepting my impulses and by learning assertive behavior to effectively communicate my true feelings to others.

*   *   *

Today I learn to gently guide my impulses to work with me in freeing myself from my old patterns of behavior.

My employing assertive behavior is a sign that I truly love and respect myself. My statements always begin with the word "I," thereby asserting my rights and beliefs. It reflects my sense of self-worth and helps me to feel secure about my values. Assertive behavior reduces my fear and anxiety as I realize that I can get my needs met and defend myself when necessary; I do not have to approach others with the fear of being hurt or controlled. I am the ruler of my own destiny and my assertive behavior demonstrates confidence in my ability to stand up for my rights. I am learning to reinforce and validate my self-esteem in my interactions with others.

*   *   *

I respect myself and enjoy standing up for my attitudes, values and beliefs.

The power to make choices in my life directly reduces my compulsive behavior. I am learning to choose situations in which I can be most effective by asserting myself. I am following the rhythm of life and observing others. Through this, I can learn when to hold out a hand and lend support, when to stand up for my rights and when to give in to others' wishes for the sake of harmony. I have my finger on the pulse of life and instinctively allow my feelings to guide my actions. I also notice that the more assertive my behavior becomes, the less inclined I am to eat or restrict food compulsively. My emotional needs are being met honestly and effectively.

*   *   *

I am learning to live from the inside out rather than being dictated to by the environment.

Affirming and accepting my body image is a two-fold process. I first commit myself to truly loving my reflection in the mirror with all its imperfections. Then I choose to understand that I am more than my reflection. My beauty comes from within and my body and my countenance reflect my sense of health and well-being. Loving myself means loving my body also. Denying my connection with my body means denying my humanity. I choose to accept myself. I find myself refreshingly open to the experiences of my body as I learn to trust it on a physiological level. I can now integrate the feelings of strength at my body's level with the knowledge and strength I am experiencing on the spiritual, psychic and emotional level.

*   *   *

When I appreciate my body and accept it, I choose to accept myself as a whole person.

I have the capacity to handle the resolution of any difficult situation I am faced with today. The more comfortable I am with myself, the more I can accept my abilities and my energy to fulfill my potential. I am determined to focus my energies on my health and my physical, mental and spiritual well-being. Loving myself is the key to remaining in tune with my abilities. I am gradually accepting that I am neither too much nor too little with regard to my abilities. I accept and enjoy pleasures through my own efforts. My body, mind and spirit join together in new ways to enrich my experience. My quest for new and better ways to live is tempered by a respect for my past and the choices I have made so far in life.

*   *   *

I accept myself and honor my ability to fulfill my potential.

My life moves forward with each step I take in the direction of wholeness. As I am true to myself, I am also true to those people in my life who are important to me. My life is enriched by my sincerity and clarity of vision. I am free to choose and my choices reflect the positive state of my being. Food is in proper perspective in my life and I am free to make other choices that further reflect my health and well-being. I continue on this path of change by affirming myself with positive self-statements. I acknowledge the continuous need to bolster my self-esteem in my daily life. I reassure myself of my recovery by my desire to nurture myself throughout this day. My life is a reflection of the positive course of my life today.

* * *

I am living each day with a renewed sense of my resiliency.

85

The universal principle of abundance influences my emotional and spiritual life. My objectivity, my flexibility and my ability to reach for new goals is a powerful force in determining my future. Each day I renew my commitment to a positive future and to expanding my resources for my own benefit and the benefit of my loved ones. I am willing to take risks and am open to new opportunities to better myself. I am a witness to the power of renewal and strength in myself. I welcome any change that will give me a deeper understanding of myself and further my process of growth. I develop my creative powers in living my daily life to the fullest.

* * *

My prosperity begins in my imagination and is reinforced by my positive actions towards myself and others.

Life flows through me and radiates the glow of my contentment with myself and my experience of life. I am continually awed by the positive forces within me that are in tune with my Higher Power's plan for my life. I now experience joy in the quiet moments of the day. I am open to seeing the rainbows after the rain and to listening to the morning sounds. The greatest joys and moments of awe-inspiring beauty occur in the wonders of nature and in the smile of another. Giving joy to others and being open to receiving the gift of love from them renews my spirit and my vitality.

* * *

I am one with myself and I rejoice in the unity that brings me peace and joy.

I notice that as I am moving through my process of growth I often visit recurring issues. I accept that this will continue until I am able to put them to rest and see them only as a memory. I focus on each issue as it presents itself in my psyche and, with loving support from others, freely discuss and experience the feeling it offers. I give myself permission to feel without the need to protect anyone except the child within me. My inner child needs these experiences in order to mature in a healthy manner. I choose to include in the new script of my life only those aspects from my past that give me joy and a feeling of safety. I create those feelings around me and manifest them in my daily life.

*   *   *

I am rewriting the script of my life and I have the privilege of choosing the context.

I visualize and honor the light of life and strength within me. I possess the capacity for wholeness and this manifests itself around me as I integrate my physical, emotional and spiritual layers. In the spirit of completion and unity, I feel at peace with my abilities and gifts. I have confidence in my inherent strength and fortitude in overcoming any obstacles I may encounter along life's way. I look to every new day with a sense of renewed vigor as I accept responsibility for my actions. I tap the intensity with which I live life to fortify me with the strength that I naturally possess. My energy moves me forward as I reach for growth in my life.

* * *

Each day brings me new awareness, feelings and memories to guide me towards peace and happiness.

My relationship with myself and with the world around me is going through a fundamental transformation. Rather than be fearful of the unknown, I trust my innate sense of timing to choose the rate at which I am changing. The process occurs as I go through my day. I have let go of the impulsive self and have accepted in its place a spontaneous and alive self which is able to choose without haste. Since I have become my own best friend and trust in the goodness of my Higher Power, I have released the pressure of the fear of deprivation. I can now relax in the promise of abundance.

*   *   *

I have taken the responsibility for my choices and feel content in the promise of abundance.

I restore the sense of balance between my inner and outer worlds, between my physical and emotional needs. I feel at peace with the balance I have created for myself. I handle the pressures of day-to-day life by relying on my innate sense of timing and my newfound ability to pace myself and take on only what I think I can realistically handle. I flow with my own personal rhythm. I know my limits. I assert myself and feel positive about taking care of my personal needs. I notice that the jobs I take upon myself are much more rewarding for me. I am free to choose my commitments and know that my efforts are directed towards their fulfillment.

*   *   *

My prime focus is on dealing with life more peacefully as I am able to monitor the pace at which I live life.

I release my expectations about myself and others in my life. By letting go of old values, I am making way for new and free-ing relationships to evolve. As I manifest myself fully, others around me feel the free-dom to relate to me in a new and refreshing way. I attract people now that I have an energy level that matches theirs. It brings me closer to where I wish to be. As I let go of old belief systems, I clear the path for the creative, self-actualizing aspect of myself to emerge. I free myself up so that I can be genuinely myself. I create a new and re-freshing way of living and relating to the world which deepens my connections to the people in my life and furthers my sense of trust in myself.

* * *

I have courageously stepped away from the preconceived notions of who I expected myself to be.

I allow the light that naturally exists within my being to have a physical manifestation today. I flow with the energy in me and encourage its expression. As I release the reins of food compulsion, I am willing to look beyond that old structure to find my delightful self — the one who loves to laugh and have others laugh with me, the one who is sensitive to others and can shed a tear for them without losing myself, the one who loves to feel the energy that only pure love can generate, the one who is free to express the creative child within and who can play with others. I am joyous and my energy is luminous and vibrant.

*   *   *

I encourage my new self to express itself today in delightful ways.

At the start of each day, I check within myself to feel my true feelings. I begin each day by acknowledging my innermost thoughts and sensations. I practice staying in tune with myself throughout the day. I accept the role food has played in my life up until now and give myself the permission, indeed, the encouragement, to feel my emotions. I am able to let go of the connection with compulsive eating or starving and with controlling those sensitive, vulnerable areas in my life. I treat myself with gentleness. It is positive for me to feel all of my feelings and to accept myself on a higher level. I master my feelings by first acknowledging them and then by expressing them when appropriate.

*　　*　　*

I allow my feelings to surface as I track them in each situation.

I accept the opportunity I now have to heal myself. I embrace the dawn of each day with this process of growing and loving myself. I come face to face with my inner beauty and consciousness. Everything about me is acceptable and worthy of acknowledgment. I welcome the changes, subtle though they seem to be. I appreciate the person who is evolving and give myself my utmost support. My loving, non-critical self welcomes the chance for a renewed life. Life flows through me as I am a channel for loving life. I love myself.

*   *   *

I reach beyond mere survival to living a life of my own design, free from restrictions.

Each feeling that I have creates an energy within me. Today I listen to the different "feeling tones" and recognize the energy they subsequently generate in my body. I am learning the special language my body speaks when I feel them. Being free from compulsive food habits allows me to understand the thoughts that bring these feelings into focus. I am befriending my body in the process. These feelings are given to me to keep me in touch with the surrounding world. They are for my protection. I am recovering the buried feelings from my past and know that the child within me used food to protect me against the intensity of my own feelings. It is safe now. I can support myself.

* * *

I acknowledge the energy that my feelings create within me.

In the process of change, I focus on those parts of myself which need to be transformed. I allow those aspects of myself which are positive and productive to my growth to become more refined. I appreciate the parts of myself which I accept and wish to keep and know that my strengths are the foundation of my personality. As I rejoice in the changes, I also rejoice in those aspects of myself that helped me and supported me in times of need. I allow my relationship with food to change and transform alongside the fundamental changes I choose to create. I am confident of my success in this process. I have confidence in myself.

*   *   *

I recognize that I can change aspects of myself that need to be transformed.

I am ready to accept that my problems with weight and food are a symptom of stress, fears or feelings of inadequacy. I am now willing to affirm myself and take the risks of exploring the many facets of my life that have led me to this point. Without being critical, I am willing to open the doors to self-discovery that will ultimately produce growth and fulfillment. I suspend my former belief system in order to make an honest evaluation and appraisal of my life. I allow myself to dream in a realistic way how I truly wish to reshape my life, beginning with changing myself. I release the fears of the past and look to this day to begin my growth.

*   *   *

I am willing to risk changing myself because I know that the end results will be positive.

My potential for growth is exciting and important to me. Developing myself to the fullest is my birthright. I accept the challenge that comes with my personal fulfillment. I take each step on the path of change with care as I truly give myself the opportunity to explore my options. I am awakening the butterfly within me that is ready to break free from its cocoon. I am allowing my secret wishes to manifest themselves daily. I surprise myself with my courage to take risks. I praise myself for my resourcefulness and am free to create the existence that I have longed for beneath my trepidation. I know that I can master whatever I choose to undertake. I am confident!

*   *   *

I am ready to create the life I want for myself with courage and resourcefulness.

As I take each step in unraveling the reasons behind my compulsive eating, I make sure that my strides are sound and sure before I take another step. I choose to travel in this unknown territory at my own speed. I feel that I have a new toy! I respect it and at the same time the thought of it thrills me at the dawn of each new day. My newfound playful attitude towards change will require real support this time. I automatically draw into my life whatever I need to become healthy. I attract supportive friends into my exciting new discoveries about myself. I am willing to share myself on a deep, meaningful level.

* * *

I release my fears in small areas and prepare my way for the larger strides that are forthcoming.

The safer I feel in my body and in my process of development, the more honest and open I am with myself and others. Fears of yesterday are no longer there and the future gets brighter each day. If there are any setbacks, I now know that they serve to fortify my process of growth because my changes are built on a firm foundation. Each time I evaluate my changes, I am elated to know that I am secure in myself and that I am able to give myself whatever I need at that moment. Yet I am able to ask for support when I need assistance and assurance. The importance of food in my life has diminished and I have developed other means to cope with my feelings.

* * *

I rely on my own capacity to meet my needs before I ask for help from others.

My life's work at this point is to search for my own individuality. It will give me the opportunity to explore the very basis of my being. In probing the depths of my self, I will choose ways to cope that will enhance my human potential. I am facing my fears and struggles to become who I have always been destined to be. I am the best I can be this day and every day. I take life as it comes. I look to the sea with its ebb and flow and know that real living is, by its very nature, dynamic, not static. I remind myself that I, too, am malleable.

* * *

While I search for the basis of my existence, I remind myself that I, too, am changeable.

My underlying psychological and spiritual relationship to the world is at the very crux of my process of transformation. As I view the world, so I live my life in it. I have chosen more effective ways to cope with the world. As I focus on my goals, I accept myself as I am now and work on the intrinsic changes that I will effect today, tomorrow and the rest of my life. In releasing the old, I embrace the opportunity to create the new from a place of awareness. I enrich my life as I probe my inner depths. I protect my right to assert myself and affirm the changing process that I experience.

*   *   *

I am pleased with my worldview which is at the core of my power to transform myself.

As I focus on my creative process of living fully and experiencing the natural sensations of my beautiful body, I notice that my intense craving for food has diminished. Where before I perceived hunger, I now feel the excitement of emotional and psychological growth. I allow myself to feel my physical sensations and experience my body along with my feelings. I feel whole, my body, mind and spirit being joined in this process of growth. My physical sensations are becoming distinctive as I experience the evolution of my total being. I am joyful as I experience being connected with my body and my feelings in the energizing movement of growth.

*   *   *

My physical relationship to the experience of change propels me to reach for new and challenging ways of living.

Joy accompanies the release of old patterns from my life. I am aware that I can never lose something that is truly mine or that is given to me by divine right. I am able to free myself from the burdens of the past and further my process of transformation more quickly than I had imagined. My eating, my attempt to find solutions to problems that were not to be solved by eating or by depriving myself of food, has left almost without notice since I have owned my right to speak up. I have made way for my self-assertion and, as if by magic, my life is falling into place.

* * *

As I address my energy to surrender my tight hold on life, it frees me up to be myself at my best.

Visualizing my healthy, vibrant body is stimulating for me. As I view my body, I am able to accept my natural body type and see that the goals I set for myself are within reach. Exercise and healthy eating habits are enough to maintain the body I wish to have. I am able to give up old views about the cultural ideal and acknowledge *my* healthy ideal as my goal. I am relieved of any burden of the past and rejoice in my ability to make positive changes in my attitude. I feel free to choose what I need for my health and know that the standards I set for myself are generated with me in mind. My values are formulated by me and are for me.

*   *   *

Today I set my own standards and values based on my own views and ideals.

I am developing a healthy, self-enhancing lifestyle. I let go of attitudes and habits that interfered with my growth and have in its place elevated my self-esteem and my connection with life. Once I have courageously stepped away from a preconceived notion of who I am, I am delighted with the new person that has emerged. My energy is refueled by my continuous motivation. I have let go of procrastination and fear and have replaced them with energizing habits. I acknowledge my successes and reward myself with something other than food. I am nurturing myself and am gentle with my body. I am stimulated by my accomplishments.

*   *   *

I allow my co-dependent patterns to disappear as I replace them with new and challenging ways of living.

I am liked and appreciated by others for my ideas, for the sense of values that I freely express and for my personality. I am enjoyable to be with and I feel comfortable in letting people know who I am. I enjoy pleasing others from a position in which I am comfortable with myself. Others support me as I allow myself to be supported and cared for. Life has taken on a fuller meaning since I am able to risk forming new, healthy relationships. When I look at myself, I like what I see, for it is a reflection of the positive course of my life today. I am able to acknowledge what others appreciate about me. I enjoy my own company and have faith in myself.

*   *   *

I choose to spend my time enriching my life with people who support my growth.

I motivate myself every day to accomplish a small goal. I channel my behavior and thoughts in a positive direction and allow negative thought patterns to quickly flow through me and exhaust themselves. The thought processes which guide my healthy attitudes towards eating, my body and my self-worth are continually focused on the positive aspects of life. I activate the healing part of myself in solving problems and in gently changing the focus of my life. The motivation for change comes from this natural movement towards health and well-being. I focus on my intrinsic desire for peace and personal fulfillment to guide my change. My goals are easily met as they are in keeping with my continuous striving for health.

* * *

I naturally allow the flow of my life to move towards health and away from former negative attitudes, values and beliefs.

I greet each new day with eagerness and anticipation. I begin by establishing my priorities and accepting a small challenge for the day. I devote my first thoughts, my morning energy, to achieving a very small goal and praise myself for it. As I set my goals, I visualize how I want to achieve them and quickly think of each step of the process. I keep my goals within reach and vary the focus of my goal-setting to keep a level of excitement in the process. I always assure myself of success by supporting each change and each new attitude and behavior. I enjoy my refreshing attitude towards life and my personal transformation.

*   *   *

I devote myself each day to setting goals, making decisions and following through with actions.

Energy breeds energy. I keep my life interesting in order to continue to stimulate myself to change. I am aware that my former compulsive behavior was my way of avoiding change. In order to keep the process of change moving in a positive direction, I vary my activities, my exercise routines and the foods I choose. I am learning to enjoy surprises and change. I choose life every time, rather than a compulsive cycle of sameness. I recognize the need for order but I am now aware that this does not necessarily translate as monotony. I feel free to introduce new ways of seeing and being. New feelings emerge, freeing me to express my level of satisfaction with my life.

*   *   *

My stability lies within myself as I learn to trust my instinctive ability to choose in my best interest.

I am able to actively choose what is happening in my life. Just as I am learning to recognize physical hunger and rewarding this newfound awareness with an appropriate choice of food, I am acknowledging my needs in every aspect of my life. My emotional and physical needs are my cues and healthy choices are my response. I no longer feel that I have to please others before I please myself. I remain aware of and respond to people's needs. However, I choose what I respond to and feel the accompanying freedom and lightness.

* * *

My trust in myself and my respect for my needs lead me to make choices that are in my best interest.

As I feed my body what I truly want to eat, I am being respectful of myself. As I please my body with special pleasures, I am being respectful of myself. I accept my sensual nature as I acknowledge my need for being touched and held. When I allow my body to be comfortable and satisfied, it generates positive energy in all aspects of my life. I am relieved of the expectations of an immature child and embrace fully the opportunity to participate in receiving fulfillment on the physical, emotional and spiritual levels. I feel on firm ground in my efforts to receive pleasure and satisfaction.

* * *

I begin with myself when I speak of love and respect.

As I look at my body, I am aware that I am changing. I am in the process of becoming exactly who I choose to be. My body is my friend. As I become more and more comfortable with myself, my body reflects these changes coming from within. I now accept my body without reservation. I manifest who I am by my self-expression and by my countenance. I befriend my physical body as I also befriend the spiritual and emotional aspects of my nature. I am pleased with who I am today and who I am becoming. I praise myself for the courage to address the issues of my body and food which need to be cleared before I am able to reach my goal of being comfortable with myself.

*   *   *

My changing relationship with my body is an indication that I am moving towards greater ease in being with myself.

114

Effecting changes in my eating habits produces positive results in each aspect of my life. I am aware that eating was a way to cope with problems. Now I am aware that with new and more effective ways to cope and actually solve my problems, I am able to live a fuller, richer life. Food simply does not taste as good as it used to and it no longer provides me with emotional comfort. I am able to enjoy my food and find that my appetite is in keeping with the amount of energy I expend. My body regulates the energy input and output very efficiently. I respect my body and treat it with the dignity it deserves.

*   *   *

I have changed the function of food in my life. It now energizes me to act in the world rather than react to situations.

I address my inner child to make sure that I keep in touch with my emotional needs each day. I notice that doing this allows me to take care of myself on a regular basis. I feel positive about this self-nurturing. Food is not a choice for this nurturing. I choose other and more effective ways to soothe my body. One example of meeting my needs is speaking up for myself rather than remaining passive. I am aware of the pattern of remaining passive and then needing to binge. I utilize my newfound ability to speak for myself to refuse food when others encourage me to eat. I also reach out to others who will listen to me rather than attempt to find misguided comfort in food.

*   *   *

Speaking for myself reduces my need for food to soothe my emotions.

I am aware that my compulsive eating involved as much pain as pleasure. Whether I ate or not, the emptiness underlying such behaviors still remained deep within my mind and spirit. Today as I release myself from the past, I am aware that the fullness of the spirit comes from within and from my spiritual connection with the Higher Power. As I continue to explore the positive aspects of life, I find that the more I accept and love myself, the more I am loved and accepted by other people. Self-love generates peace within and contentment at this stage of my life.

*   *   *

I am a part of all the goodness that has been created in the world because I am a part of the Higher Power by my belief and trust.

I am a magnet for love, success and happiness. My self-image generates confidence with those I meet. Good things regularly come into my life. My relationships are long-lasting and all my projects are carried to completion. As my self-perception continues to grow, I am able to demonstrate positive attitudes and results in all areas of my life. I focus on my potential each day as I awake. I de-emphasize my shortcomings and understand that both strength and weakness complete my humanity. I compare myself to no one so that I may focus on my own best qualities and continually enhance my self-worth.

* * *

My life is a reflection of my positive attitudes today.

I have all that I require to realize my dreams. Focusing on my positive goals brings them closer to me each day. Clarifying my goals ensures my success. I visualize my success in a vivid image. I see myself exuding self-confidence and self-acceptance. These inspire me to reach continually for bigger goals and to attain all that I desire. I am able to approach a difficult challenge with poise and confidence. Envisioning my higher good enables me to strive to fulfill the potential that I have been given by the Higher Power.

*   *   *

Each day I renew my commitment to a positive future and to expanding my resources to attain it.

Breaking away from others' expectations is a liberating factor in self-discovery. I am comfortable with myself in all situations because I know and accept who I am today and who I am striving to be. When I am in a group of people, I make every attempt to contribute to the good of the whole rather than trying to be the center of everyone's attention in positive or negative ways. My personal discovery of who I am and my expression of my true self bring positive results into my daily life. Truly knowing myself allows me to freely express my feelings and beliefs without the pressure to conform. I am assured that my independence is of value to myself and to others in my life.

* * *

I am true to my instincts and feel a new warmth in my social contacts as people respond positively to the real me.

I capitalize on my potential. By breaking the compulsive habits around food, exercise or other rituals, I am expressing my strength and my will to live rather than to merely survive. Living means to embrace life fully. I ardently develop my talents and abilities to carry me to the highest possible achievement. Self-confidence is a by-product of my expression in the world, whether it is a tangible thing, human contact or simply goodwill towards others. I gain by giving and expressing myself. My happiness and self-confidence come from within me and are expressed in the world through my actions.

*   *   *

I gain in self-confidence as I employ my potential fully to express myself in life.

121

One aspect of self-acceptance necessary for my personal growth is flexibility. Full recovery implies healthy flexibility. I am able to bend and apply new principles to my life to meet each situation. I am aware that what works for me may not be appropriate for everyone. I am able to accept what may be best for another. A healthy interdependence is the flexibility I wish for myself. I can express myself and still be connected in a positive meaningful manner with my loved ones. I choose to be a part of others' lives and recognize more of my self-worth through my own actions and by helping others discover their own uniqueness.

*   *   *

I fully experience my values in life through my flexibility in my relationships with others.

My courage is manifested in my ability to confront myself and my secrets. As I bring light into the darkness of my eating behavior, I let another part of me experience freedom. My body image is the first aspect of my personality to manifest this change. My weight may stay the same, but the life that exists inside in the form of self-acceptance has a way of showing in my every expression. I walk with more confidence and slowly accept my biological destiny, the body type that goes along with my wonderful heritage. I visualize my ideal body with very gradual changes. My health is of prime importance when I consider changing my outer body.

*   *   *

My positive feelings help mold my body image and encourage me to express myself to the fullest.

The true purpose of my life is to matter to myself and to others, to stand for something worth living for. I am committed to releasing the negative hold that compulsive eating behavior has had on my life and the lives of those around me. I accept responsibility for my past actions, so that I can fully enjoy the new life I am building for myself. Releasing my judgments about myself allows me to blossom and bask in the warm rays of my healthy self-love. I can say yes to the things I wish for in life and no to the things that are not in my best interest. I am awed by my power and assert myself daily.

*　　　*　　　*

I create my new life illuminated by my inner light and accept the scrutiny of my loving self.

I acknowledge my need to continue with the process of growing and affirming myself. I embrace the opportunity to build my sense of self-worth and to put my plans for growth into action. I accept the up-and-down process of change and dwell only on the positive aspects while I learn from my past. I accept my humanity and know that perfection is an unrealistic goal. I change what is possible for me to change and accept what I cannot change. I thank the Higher Power for the gifts I have and see my shortcomings as lessons to be learned. I support my own efforts by setting realistic short-term goals and by clarifying my goals on a daily basis.

*   *   *

I look on my shortcomings with the realism of an adult rather than the demanding nature of a child.

Centering myself is my goal for today. By getting to my deepest level of feeling, I come to know myself better and am able to be spontaneous and alive. Knowing my center, I am able to cope and to function from a place of security and liveliness. I become more aware of my strength and my creativity as well as my true feelings when I allow myself to get in touch with my center. It is my sense of internal consistency that gives me what I need to live fully. I replenish and nurture myself with food for my spirit each time I go within to the cache of gifts that empower me. I receive the gifts from the Higher Power and utilize them to the best of my ability.

*   *   *

As I affirm my center, I touch the aspect of myself that radiates energy and joy.

Finding my own voice is my goal for today. I look deep within myself beyond expectations and criticism to find what I truly want to say. I make my personal statement in my own words, actions and dress, with a vitality that shines through me. I replace the passive need for food, which once muted my personal expression, with the newfound voice in which I make my needs known. This voice has always been with me but was not free to speak until now. I am spontaneously alive as I effectively express myself. What I have to say is important. I value my opinions and move into the future with an emphasis on open communication.

*   *   *

I give myself permission to speak, knowing that what I say is important.

Each person has a different rhythm. I find my own rhythm and move with it rather than against it. It reinforces my energy. I am able to listen to my own internal rhythms and take cues from my body to eat only when I am hungry. My body signals to me when other physical needs such as the need for touch and physical closeness are asking to be met. I am learning to differentiate the various needs I have, be they emotional, spiritual or physical. I honor my physical needs and recognize that food is only one such need. I love my body and treat it with respect. I give my body healthy food and allow myself to enjoy the experience of satiety. My rhythms are unique to me and I honor them.

* * *

I reinforce my energy when I move with my own rhythm.

As I evolve and grow I set my sights on the light at the end of the tunnel. My feet are firmly planted on the ground, in the present; however, I always keep my eyes on the goals I have set for myself. With each stage of growth come new surprises and new challenges. My problem with food has changed and I am now aware of the underlying issues I have avoided facing. The patterns of avoidance are no longer of use to me. Once I accept the awareness with which I am blessed today, my resistance to change melts away along with the fear of the unknown. My knowledge of myself is my newfound strength as I willingly plunge into the depths of my spirit. I am rich with the gifts of my strengths and abilities.

*   *   *

I am soothed by my ability to overcome my resistance and confront issues when I am ready to handle them.

I am a part of all that I meet along life's way. The people in my life are sent to me and I to them for purposes beyond my present vision. I value them and the gifts we bring each other. I am willing to learn from them and to accept what they have to offer me. I am ready to trust, to go out on a limb to learn what I can from the people I meet. I am also able to move on from relationships that are no longer healthy for me. I cannot be there for everyone and I am willing to accept my own limitations as well as the limitations of others. I am true to myself and to the process of my growth.

* * *

I let go of my defenses and judgments to be able to listen in an enlightened way.

As each night ends and the dawn signals the beginning of a new day, I await the beginning of each new stage of growth and a letting go of maladaptive patterns. I know that when the space around and inside me is the darkest and the bleakest, the new light and the new way of being are coming soon. Rather than give up at this point, I allow myself to experience what I am struggling with. As I am ready to move forward, I allow the behaviors to change and gradually step into the gray light of dawn. As I become more sure of myself in my new way of life, I bask in the strong light of knowing. I am comfortable and reassured yet again in the act of knowing myself.

*   *   *

I am comfortable and reassured as I bask in the light of a new beginning.

I recognize the situations and signposts that may create a relapse in my recovery. Fatigue and emotional stress are times I am vulnerable. Giving myself away is also a time when I am most likely to revert to old patterns of eating. Becoming too rigid in my diet creates deprivation and allows the return of old behaviors. Allowing others to control my life and acquiescing to the forceful demands of others when I am ambivalent about their requests is a key factor in my relapse and return to food as a friend. I am searching for a balance in my life and gradually becoming aware of my internal cues that signal a warning not to respond and continue to fulfill the old, comfortable roles.

*   *   *

I am coming to rely on my internal signals as an indication that it is time for prevention and pulling back from my activities and involvement with others.

As I reflect on my past eating patterns, I am able to alter my relationship with food. I am ready to accept my feelings about food with all of the added shame and release the past in order to move into the present. I move into the present feeling very alive and aware of my goals and my attributes. I am allowing new thoughts to enter my mind as I release negative thought patterns and the behaviors that went with them. In releasing the past, I am gradually freeing myself from feelings of failure and reinforce my successful behaviors with positive, uplifting thoughts. Each affirming thought moves me into the light and away from the bondage of food.

* * *

I am in possession of myself, free to make decisions to change any behavior or thought that impedes my progress.

I am integrating the masculine and feminine sides of my personality. As I grow and change, it is necessary for me to accept all the feelings I have and be willing to express them to others. I am now giving credence to both sides of my personality — the passive, maternal side and the active, masculine side. The marriage of the masculine and the feminine within me brings me peace and fosters the completion of my personality. As I express the masculine and the feminine, I am aware of my different body parts coming alive and becoming more defined. My body gradually changes with my new personal expression and I acknowledge the integration by allowing these changes to occur.

*   *   *

I move towards active living as I synthesize the masculine and feminine aspects of my personality.

My body grows in vitality as I successfully release my former conditioned responses in relating to it. As my body becomes more alive, I am aware of my own life-force, the energy within me that encourages me to grow and move on. My natural energy is like a circuit moving through my body, giving me cues as to where it is blocked. As I become more aware of my body, I am able to free the energy blocks and foster greater ease in my movement. I find myself being drawn to explore different ways of moving which encourage my energy flow, whether it be through dance, yoga or simple movement exercises. I am careful not to overextend myself in exercise, but to gradually allow myself to evolve.

*　　*　　*

I am encouraging my body to move the same way I would encourage a child to explore the novelty of running, jumping and skipping.

As I cultivate my internal world for my growth and acceptance of myself, I am able to project my aura in the external world. I encourage myself to be introspective and experiential in my quest for peace. I am aware of the interplay between emotions and actions and pleased with my internal evolution. I view my inner world as a road-map with many roads and major thorough-fares connecting my feelings and energy fields. Both physical and emotional energy can be transformed into the force behind my growth and actualization. This possibility excites me and encourages me to become fully aware of myself as I grow and change.

*   *   *

I involve my total being in my self-expression as I combine my physical and emotional energies.

As I reach within myself, I come into contact with the pure emotions that yearn for expression. Through years of suppression and hiding, I have pushed my real feelings into the dark recesses of my mind. As I illuminate the darkness with awareness and growth, I am more in touch with the motivating factors behind my eating patterns. I look within myself for the answers to my problems, for now I am fully aware that they lie within me. I look to others for support but I look to myself to be the impetus to change. I relate to myself as I would to my best friend, with compassion and patience. I am grateful for the insight which I am blessed with at this time.

*   *   *

I look within myself for the impetus to my evolution and change which will propel me into the future.

When I encourage myself to relax, I allow my thoughts to parade before me. I am able to sort through my conscious thoughts and separate the positive self-enhancing thoughts from the negative self-deprecating ones. The states of feeling associated with the positive thoughts are light and freeing while the feelings associated with the negative thoughts are heavy and binding. I consciously choose to have the positive self-statements and thoughts in my life today and always. The cyclical negative self-statements are replaced by those that are positive and supportive in nature. I choose mental health and wellness.

*   *   *

As I continue to explore the positive aspects of life, I no longer have a place for negative habits.

My attachment to the psychological comforts that food used to give me is sometimes
outside my awareness. My yearning for the
earlier pleasant feelings of security creates
an anxiety as I consider giving up my attachment to food. On a conscious level I know
that food does not satisfy the yearning any
longer. I must have something which takes
the place of the need for food, rather than
my giving up food itself. I replace this
yearning with building my sense of self,
with love and appreciation for my being.
Although sometimes this is a difficult love, I
reach within to know myself and I have
confidence that the love will come. I am
comfortable and secure within myself.

*   *   *

*I release my apprehension about not getting
enough food and instead fill myself with love.*

My ability to become flexible allows me to increase my independence and my sense of self-worth. In order to release feelings of dependence on rituals, habits, food and people, I must replace them with feelings of strength and a healthy detachment from substances and people in my environment. Becoming more detached encourages me to have a broader view of life and my place in it. Interdependence is my ultimate goal, with this phase of detachment allowing me to choose the degree of closeness and distance with which I wish to relate to others. It helps me further to maintain a proper perspective on food and its role in my life. I befriend food as I befriend the significant people in my life, treating each one with respect.

*   *   *

Today I welcome detachment as the path to interdependence.

The function of food in my life must gradually be coordinated and integrated into a greater schemata for my growth. Shifting the focus away from food and my attachment to it frees me to choose a new path to follow. My resources seem endless. As I try to narrow my choices, I notice that I limit myself and my relationship to the world. Opening myself up to the possibilities that lie before me rejuvenates my spirit. I focus on the center of my being for an anchor as I explore novel ways of living. In this period of experimentation, I am ready to taste freedom, knowing that I will eventually choose a new path which will give me the direction and focus I need.

*   *   *

I affirm my goals by repeating them to myself and choosing a new path in the direction of wholeness.

As I explore the world of my images, dreams, daydreams and fantasies, I am awed by the richness, vitality and luminescence of my inner world. Allowing myself to feel and see what really lies within me positively reinforces my quest for confidence and peace. I feel ready to express my richness and have this manifested in my life. I continually praise the Higher Power for helping me in keeping this clear world of images alive while I attempted to drown them out. This inner world has the feelings of childhood with all its innocence. I am tapping the pure feelings of childhood to regain my connection with the world of images and hope.

* * *

As I explore my inner world, I am ready to allow its richness to manifest in my life today.

It is indeed possible for me to soar to the loftiest heights. Each day I feel reinforced by my small successes and my newfound attitudes towards myself. I am tapping my strength and find that it is my greatest asset. Holding on to my old patterns is no longer an option for me since I have now experienced a level of vitality I intend to nurture and pursue. I am rich with all I need to get me through any difficulty in life. I have proven my resiliency. I have fulfilled all my duties towards others and feel the freedom to devote time to myself. Renewing my spirit will positively affect me and all those who are part of my life.

*   *   *

I appreciate the person who is evolving and devote my nurturing energies towards myself.

When I want to overeat or restrict my food, I will give myself five minutes to process what it is that I am avoiding feeling. After the waiting period, I will give myself permission to have the food I wanted. I tell myself that it is healthy for me to eat. I choose not to binge because I want to be aware of my feelings. As I give myself permission to eat, I do not have to hide or sneak the food I want. I am cautious enough to stop eating before I am too full and I allow myself to digest the food slowly. I am pleased with my body when I respond to my cues to eat. I am going with the flow of my body as I recover.

*   *   *

I trust my body to signal hunger and to give me the feedback about satiety and the presence of feelings.

I express my energy and vitality in all that I do. I am an individual who projects my internal magnetism in simple everyday acts. I value myself and in turn respect others. I appreciate others for both their differences and likenesses. What I learn from others I am able to weave into the richness of my own life. I contribute to others from a place of wholeness; that is my greatest asset. By exploring my depths, I have more to offer the world. I am more truly myself now than I was previously able to be. I accept myself and that is the basis for any growth. I acknowledge my uniqueness and express that to the fullest of my being.

*   *   *

Interacting with people increases my energy and allows me to freely express my own uniqueness.

I enjoy initiating ideas and following them through to completion. I complete projects effortlessly and take pride in my accomplishments. I am aware that my act of completion is a reflection of my level of commitment to any project or relationship. I enjoy having the stamina and fortitude to carry my ideas and projects to fruition; only then can I witness the fullness of my ability to follow through. I strive to be at my best in all that I do and I am aware of my effectiveness in the world. I can see the results of my commitment to breaking my compulsive eating patterns in all aspects of my daily life. I am the living proof of my success!

*   *   *

I notice that my level of commitment is the backbone of any undertaking that I choose.

When I search for another's approval and deny my own right to express myself, I give myself away. I take the opportunity to change this pattern now that I am aware of its detrimental effect on the quality of my life. I vow to work actively in my personal and professional relationships to express myself appropriately. Asserting myself reinforces my belief in myself and in my natural rights as an individual. Each interaction in which I assert myself adds one more piece to secure the foundation of my self-esteem. I honor and respect myself and it is time that I show this to the world. I am my own personal vision of honest expression.

* * *

My personal expression allows me to publicly acknowledge my respect for myself.

147

In the process of growth, I am willing to take risks. If in this process I make a mistake, I am able to learn from it and recognize that I am growing. I rejoice in my ability to learn from my errors. I choose to focus on the positive lessons I have learned and release any criticism that I begin to engage in towards myself and my actions. I am no longer striving for perfection nor am I willing to sacrifice the true value of lessons I have learned merely for appearances. I am actively working now to learn and grow. I am in the process of evolving and I see each day as a privilege to direct my own metamorphosis.

*   *   *

I look forward to the day when the errors I make in this stage of my evolution will be a part of my history.

I am setting out today to further develop my talent and confirm my purpose in life. I focus on what I do well and go about the day reinforcing this strength in all that I do. I am grateful for my talents and for my ability to apply them in a meaningful way. I notice that my unique cluster of abilities is more readily available to me now that I am able to release my preoccupation with food, diet and weight. My mind is clear and I am able to focus my energy on more fulfilling enterprises. I continually refine my relationship with food in much the same way that I explore my potential. I challenge myself to reach realistic goals of personal expression and success.

*   *   *

I vow to become my personal best in all that I do.

I deserve to get what I want from life. When I go with the flow of the day, my life has less struggle. I am able to focus on my goals and participate fully in each day. Trying to fit everything into neat little boxes creates resistance around me and around others in my life. When I can sit back and not structure my time and events, I find that there is less resistance and consequently less struggle in my life as a whole. I create free space in which to observe life and to feel life's effects on me. I am then ready to choose how I wish to participate in life.

* * *

I have gone beyond struggling with the details of life and my life has taken on a certain rhythm which allows me to make decisions freely.

Recharging myself from my center is my goal for today. By getting in touch with my center, I am getting in touch with the deepest level of my feelings. I allow the vibrations to come to the surface so that I can pay close attention to the messages of my body. As I befriend my body in the process of recovery, I become more aware of my strength, my creativity, as well as the nature of my true feelings. I release the power that outer influences have over my thoughts and feelings as I touch the center of my being. I fulfill my potential as I contact and validate my true self. By knowing myself, I am able to share myself with the world.

*   *   *

I accept the stability and strength that come from contacting and replenishing my spirit.

Happiness is its own reward. I have learned much from the search for my true self. I utilize my talents on this search to contact the Higher Power. I have set positive goals in my life and have concentrated on these goals until they have been fulfilled. As I strived to accomplish my purpose in life, I have remained true to myself and allowed myself to be flexible. Through focusing on my personal development, I have enhanced my strengths. I am utilizing my personal power to the fullest as I claim my position in the complex pattern of life.

*   *   *

I soar to the greatest heights as I feel myself grow and direct my energies towards a purposeful goal.

I bring a happy, fulfilled person into my relationships. I release the old structure and establish a sense of exploration. If I feel controlled or if I feel the need to control, I immediately become aware of the question that needs to be asked of myself or others. The question will clarify the momentary confusion in our ability to express our true selves. When I feel a need to perform, I become stuck in a set pattern of interacting in which I am reacting in the present just as I did in a similar situation in the past. My happy fulfilled self brings a fresh look to each situation and to each relationship.

* * *

As I interact from a space of consent and freedom, I am aware of the many possibilities that exist in each relationship.

Shifting my energy in the direction of my inner life moves me into my personal reality. I accept my identity. I choose to focus on the life-giving force within me. I choose the transformative process and remove my attention from food and appearance as I undertake this journey. I remind myself that I can return to my known self anytime. I can choose to keep the patterns that I have now or I can choose to change them. I am willing to suspend familiar beliefs for newer values that may help me with my compulsive patterns around food. I am grateful for the opportunity to grow and develop a new and different attitude towards life in general and towards food in particular.

* * *

I can choose what I want to change.

Focusing on my inner reality and my feelings about my body allows me to stop eating when I am full. I rely on my responses, my connection to all things living. I participate fully in life when I am able to heed the internal signals of my body. Obeying cues outside of myself when I am full or hungry denies my participation in my own sustenance and nurturance. I then allow my body to become an object and remove the humanity from my own process. No matter what my past relationship was with my body, the time to acquaint myself with my basic connection with life is now. I am free to acknowledge my body. I am grateful to the Higher Power that continues to give me signals to guide me in this life. I am grateful to my body as it continues to feel.

* * *

I commit myself to the process of discovery each minute I feel a body signal whether it is pleasure or pain.

The more I struggle, the more out of control my life is. The more I focus on food as the source of all problems in my life, the more out of touch I am with my inner reality, my world of feelings. When I release the struggle with food and know that the truth and the answers lie within myself, I feel a certain calm flow outward from the center of my being and release the tension between my body and food. No matter how many times I have tried to release food as the central problem, I have in the past focused on depriving myself of the substance which was originally the solution to my problems. Food then became a problem in itself. I now allow my body and my feelings to communicate with each other, knowing that I am one.

*　　*　　*

I now acknowledge both my internal and external needs.

Reviewing my life up to now increases my fortitude in ending my battle with food. I have survived, no, more than survived, I have lived my life and endured whatever was in my path. My issues with food are now within my control. Food was my answer to all my problems and I was not sure what was on the other side. I am now ready to look at this and the purpose that food served in my life. I will ask food what I am trying to get from it when I overeat or restrict. I am changing just by considering the possibility of releasing this energy in my life. I approach an old problem with a fresh viewpoint. I am ready for transformation.

* * *

No matter how much I may feel out of control, I am in charge of my life and my issues with food.

I am allowing those aspects of myself which I have cut off and have hid from others to come to the fore now. I am able to ask. I am able to receive. I can take risks knowing that I can always retreat to my old defenses. Eventually, I know that I will no longer need them. I can take a few steps forward and, as I learn to trust myself and others, my risks will be greater and my strides longer. I am willing to go through the process of growth so that the slower parts can catch up with the parts of myself that have grown up more. I look forward to integrating all aspects of my life. Today is the beginning of this growth cycle.

* * *

I am allowing myself to have needs and to catch up on my growth.

The inner part of myself is the feeling part. The outer part is my logical or thinking part. I am working to bring these two components together to form a complete whole. I can join these two parts by expressing my feelings instead of eating or restricting. I am willing to risk sharing this aspect with someone who will listen and support my process of change. I risk exploring my feelings a little at a time. I notice that my confidence builds with each shared feeling. I plan to continue sharing until I have explored my inner self and feel it unite with my outer logical self. All parts of my being, my thoughts and feelings are acceptable to me and others.

*   *   *

I am grateful for the trust I am able to share with others.

All parts of me are compatible. I release all conflicts which interfere with my growth. I accept that I may disagree with others and still be acceptable to myself. I know that being agreeable at all times is not possible if I am going to give myself permission to grow and change. I accept this and welcome the change that comes along with my personal expression. My individuality is special and is worth sharing. My personal characteristics and qualities are unique to me and that is a positive aspect of my specialness. I like myself and am my own best friend, supporting my newfound abilities and personal expression.

* * *

I am willing to risk being myself and noncompliant if that helps my personal development.

Hope, understanding, self-respect and regard for others are all components of my personal growth. All these characteristics are natural consequences of asking questions of myself and my past. I know improvements have occurred when any one of the above qualities is dominant in my thinking. Allowing these ideas to take over my thoughts generates more positive thoughts and feelings. My circular compulsive thoughts are replaced by thoughts with a freshness and lightness that is in itself reinforcing. I enjoy my quest for truth and happiness which naturally follow when I am true to myself and respect my process of growth.

* * *

Asking questions of myself has freed me to express myself in positive ways.

I focus on the positive health-producing aspects of my body rather than on an illusive ideal. I think of all the wonderful things my body can do, the functional and creative aspects of movement and health. My body has put up with past mistreatment and I thank it for surviving. I no longer have to compromise my body's full expression to satisfy the side of me that is rigid. I call on the image-creating side of me and evoke positive healthy pictures of my body in my mind each day. I ignore any negative self-statement by turning it into a positive statement about my body. Positive thoughts and attitudes help create positive feelings about my body's image.

* * *

I promote my body's health by focusing on its positive aspects rather than on the ideal body.

I feel stronger today and am willing to face the feelings I have been keeping away from my awareness. I deal with food as a friend and greet it peacefully as I approach each meal. Food nourishes me and keeps me alive. I am ready to release myself from my self-imposed food rituals and risk building a new life. As I look behind my defensive behavior, I come face to face with my vulnerable self, the part of me that needs to be nurtured and reparented. I allow myself time to unfold all the issues that need to be addressed and trust my unique sense of timing in this process of self-discovery. I am lovable in every part of myself.

* * *

I like all aspects of myself and welcome the unique opportunity to have an intimate relationship with myself.

As I increase my awareness of myself, I am ready to approach my body as a safe place to live. I trust my body. I begin this process with the awareness of hunger. I am learning which signals are hunger signals and to respond to them when appropriate. I am pleased when I am aware of my physiological need for food. Life is brighter on days when I am synchronous with my body. I allow myself to receive the nurturance I need, both from myself and from others. I am willing to take responsibility for myself and my actions and to be aware when I may slip back into old patterns with food and behavior. I can acknowledge the feelings quickly and get through any setback with my self-esteem intact. I am coming from a place of trust and nurturance.

* * *

I am willing to take responsibility for myself and my actions and to be aware when I may slip back into old patterns with food and behavior.

My motivation for change is self-love. I realize that when, in the past, I was motivated to change from a viewpoint of dissatisfaction with my body and myself, I was never very successful. This time, I repeat to myself daily, "I Love You" and truly mean it. I say it over and over to myself, just as I would to a small child who is injured and looks to me for reassurance that everything will be okay. My inner self needs the reassurance and knowledge that I am growing and getting healthier each day. As I allow time for my vulnerable and worldly selves to merge, I release any tendency towards impatience and replace it with feelings of unconditional love.

* * *

I am encouraging the integration of my inner vulnerable self with the outer, more worldly self.

The aura around my body reflects my positive feelings about myself. I am working on recognizing my positive energy and harnessing it for my growth and self-discovery. I notice that when I am feeling positive, I am more resilient and able to handle life's small pressures. When I am not, my structure seems to break down and the smallest slight seems monumental. I reinforce my strengths each day and set realistic, step-by-step goals that will bolster my weaker qualities. I will always have boundaries, yet when I am stronger, I enjoy the way I can make my own decisions and choose the influences in my life. I appreciate each step I take on the way towards wholeness.

*　　*　　*

I am able to have flexible yet protective boundaries around myself.

It is within my power to change my attitude towards my weight, my eating and my body image. By continually picturing myself as satisfied and happy with the body I have now, I will eventually fulfill that prophecy. I am able to change my beliefs about my eating by continually reinforcing the positive habits I have already acquired and by reducing my investment in unhealthy eating habits. It is the latter that will keep me hooked into the old maladaptive patterns. Believing in my ability to change is the key to my success and happiness. I am willing to take the risk in believing in my healthy self.

*   *   *

Being present in my various stages of growth is essential to keep the momentum of going forward.

Ah, The Brick Wall! How many times have I come to this point in the change process and chosen to stay the same? It is at this point that I sometimes give up. I now know that there are many choices when I face my deepest fears. I can go over the brick wall, around it, cut a path through it or I can retreat. The choice is mine and mine alone. I know deep down that it is myself that I have feared. Maybe I am not as fearful as I have previously thought but I will never know until either I make a commitment to change or accept staying the same. This is the time to face myself honestly and to gradually learn to be content with myself. I am ready to accept myself in every way.

*   *   *

I am the only person who can decide whether to make a difference in my life or choose to stay the same.

How do I give myself love that I have never truly received or have not been aware enough to see in another's eyes? I begin by gently touching my body, soothing myself as I would soothe someone I love. I allow myself to take in the love I give my body. I practice what it feels like to receive love. I continue to touch my arm or face until I can truly feel the caring involved. I receive the energy and the intent of giving and receiving love. Taking away from my consciousness any negative thoughts and judgments about my body is essential during this exercise. I continue to do this until all of my negative thoughts are washed from my consciousness.

*   *   *

I soothe myself by focusing on the sensations and intend to give myself love and receive it.

I reward myself for my assertive behavior. I focus on my successful interactions and release my fears about rejection because of my ability to stand up for myself. I direct my energy to my healthy development. I know that my strength will attract stronger people to support me but not to hold me up. I shall stand tall and feel my strength as I sense the rightness within my body. My feelings of strength and my assertive movements allow me the self-expression I desire. I communicate assertiveness and the feeling of that inalienable right to express myself.

* * *

My consistency in practicing assertive behavior is the key to getting effective results in my interactions with others.

I am the harbinger of change. I bring to myself and those I interact with a new sense of peace and honesty. I am in the process of changing my orientation to the world. I have the ability to reinforce my strengths and to de-emphasize my lesser qualities. I face life realistically with both feet on the ground and with my eye towards the future. My change comes from deep within my spirit. I have the ability to shed my old belief system and to replace unproductive thoughts with positive, productive ones. I marshal all of my energy to see my Higher Self and to feel the positive vibrations of my metamorphosis.

* * *

My openness to change is the cherished gift I give to myself.

I bring balance back into my life. I de-emphasize my attachment to food, broaden my interests and search for pleasure and reward in new and different ways. I desire and actively search for more self-knowledge and understanding of my thoughts and feelings. I look to my body for answers and patiently wait for the simplicity of the process to bring buried information to the surface. In releasing my hold on the past and by bringing memories to the light, I experience increased energy, vitality and self-appreciation. In the process of letting go and grieving past hurts, I begin to feel the lightness in my body and rejoice at the opportunity for renewal.

*   *   *

I am witness to the power of renewal and strength in myself.

I have nothing to fear in this world once I am in possession of myself. I am able to liberate myself by choosing self-acceptance and support for all my efforts. I feel the unity of my feelings, my body and my spirit as I am able to face emotional situations without the need to use food, either by over-eating or by depriving myself. I feel a new sense of maturity and self-efficacy as I am able to assert myself and express my feelings in a positive and protective way. I no longer need food; truly, my need has diminished with my continued growth and greater self-awareness. I look with joy upon my ability to nurture myself in creative ways.

*   *   *

Self-confidence is a by-product of expressing myself in the world and breaking my patterns of passivity.

I have my own power and energy. I am able to express this in the world through my work and my ability to relate positively to others. I express my commitment when I am committed, for I have a true desire to please myself rather than to go on pleasing others. I wish to develop myself to my full capacity. I am amazed to discover the untapped energy that lies within me. I had put myself on hold and now I am ready to harness the stored-up energy and direct it towards a positive goal. Being able to focus on my successful completion of any project is in itself fulfilling. I am tapping my creative source and exploring my personal vitality and dynamic energy.

*　　*　　*

I look to the intensity with which I live life today to reinforce the strength and energy I naturally possess.

I focus on the positive aspects of the past I wish to take with me and release the nonproductive and maladaptive behavior patterns I wish to leave behind. As I do this, I feel the weight gradually shift in my body and notice that my emphasis is more on making my upper body stronger and releasing the weight held in my lower body. My energy is expressed in the lightness with which I move and the joy and presence that come from the center of my being. I feel the resolution that comes with letting go and the excitement that comes with discovery. My mind is at peace and my body manifests that peacefulness and integration at its core. My mind and body are unified.

*   *   *

I am lighter and freer in my body.

Spiritual Nurturance

I recognize the need for nurturance at the very core of my being. I am pleased when I am able to nurture myself adequately and feel at peace with myself. I reflect on those moments as I make a mental note of the similarities between various circumstances. I remember the bodily feelings, the thoughts I was thinking and the spiritual connection that I felt with the universe. I recall the feeling of being in the flow of life rather than working against the flow. Those feelings of oneness are felt at the core of my being. As I reflect on those times or imagined experiences, I am able to bring forth, through my breathing and the rhythmic movement of my body, the constellation of feelings I experience in the present.

*   *   *

I replenish and nurture myself each time I go within.

Each day as I wake, I begin with my own chosen words of inspiration. I start the day renewed and resolved to continue removing compulsive patterns from my life. As I go through the day, I continue to reinforce my positive beliefs when I encounter obstacles and especially if I return momentarily to old behavior patterns. I remind myself that each moment is only a moment in time and that a past moment does not necessarily have to influence future moments. I remain forward-reaching at all times. The mark of change is the ability to separate events and not to allow one momentary lapse to influence the rest of the day or the rest of my life. Each day is a new day and each moment or event is new.

* * *

I can change each moment to reinforce a goal I have set for the day.

I establish a strong foundation upon which I choose to grow and learn. I create what is needed in my life. I recognize the need to build and support myself from the bottom up just as I would in building a home. I work with the foundation and the internal systems prior to dealing with the external appearance and providing the finishing touches. My attention initially is devoted to the foundation and structure which will support my internal and external beauty. My difficulty with compulsive eating appears to be about my body weight and external appearance, yet through this process of growth I am aware of the internal feelings which need to be addressed first.

* * *

I commit myself to rebuilding the foundation of my life as a prelude to making internal and external changes.

In my growth process, I am becoming aware that changes are made in different stages, not in one overall transformation. It is analogous to a butterfly coming out of the cocoon. The end result takes time and the peeling of the layers brings surprises as the metamorphosis gradually unfolds. I accept myself in each stage, reinforcing the belief that the process is the goal. Learning to live and accept myself is my focus at each stage. The growth in each area of my change takes place at its own rate. I direct my energy to living in the present moment. I put one foot in front of the other and one positive thought in the place of a negative thought as I continue to support my efforts to grow and change.

* * *

I manifest my positive belief system through my actions at every stage of growth.

I release my remorse over yesterday and all of the other yesterdays when I ate compulsively. I have a positive self-regard for myself today and always. I release my criticism of any and all of my behavior regarding food. I renew this forgiveness each day, whether the sun is shining and I feel positive about myself or it is raining outside and I encounter the darkness within my soul. I accept each part of myself and see the past as an event which needs healing and understanding from me before I can release it completely. While I am healing, I feel the changes and the peace growing inside me. I accept myself. I have the insight and the ability to change my life.

*   *   *

I heal myself by accepting and understanding the past rather than feeling remorse over it.

I am my own ally. My feelings about my body from the inside are my directors in recovery. If my feelings have been discounted by others and I have become afraid to express them, it will take care and consideration to bring them forth. I will take time to allow my feelings to surface. I will trust myself and my feelings in every area of my life. I acknowledge my emotions. I listen to what my body is saying and what my thoughts are that either complement or conflict with my body sensations and emotions. I trust that I will be able to deal with all the feelings that emerge.

*   *   *

My feelings are part of myself and I welcome the opportunity to enrich my knowledge of myself on a deep emotional level.

My criticisms of myself serve me in un-suspecting ways. If I continue to stay on the merry-go-round of elation at compliments and depression at self-criticism, then I avoid dealing with the real issues beneath my eating and continual rejection. I ask myself what this cycle is keeping me from facing and what the comfort — albeit negative — of compulsive patterns is. If compulsions are taking the place of love, then I am reinforcing my inability to experience love. I have the faith and stamina to overcome my compulsion. I am ready to come out of hiding so that I can truly get to know myself and share my beauty and uniqueness with others.

* * *

I am free to remove the cloak of denial to face the openness that is anxious to be discovered.

I have a limitless capacity to enjoy life. I engage my brain to utilize all the facts I have accumulated throughout my search for health. I explore the emotional and holistic side of my mind to reach the level of awareness necessary to move me into the health I seek. I can have it. I work toward an integrated mind, body and spirit. I love the person I am becoming. I am in full possession of my sense of self and my level of joy increases daily. I am in touch with my Higher Power as I achieve this goal of synthesis on my journey towards truth and self-awareness.

* * *

I praise my Higher Power for giving me the capacity and awareness to feel life so intensely.

I know who I am by the friends I keep. I have chosen them to be in my life for certain reasons. I have a desire to see everyone grow with me and support my growth. Some will be able to do this; for others, it may be asking too much of them at this time. I release my connection with them in order to seek the support I need at this time of transition. This does not mean that I care for them any less; I must care about myself more now and in a way that is different from before. I have embarked on a journey and I am committed to the process. There is no magic in it, only an integrative power which is the product of my own imagination. I can become what I believe I can be.

*   *   *

I choose those friends in my life today who can help me discover my uniqueness.

Abundance manifests itself in every area of my life. I have friends and support. I enjoy good health. Joy is there for the taking. I am able to remove the veil of unhappiness and see what is on the other side. Getting through the layers of awareness enables me to see into the future and to mobilize my energy in positive directions. I am grateful for and honored by the life I lead. I thank the Higher Power for the guidance that has led me to this place in life and for helping me in good times and in bad. In my heart of hearts, I have always known that I was loved by someone greater than myself. Knowing this Loving Presence has given me the encouragement to love myself.

*   *   *

I see myself with increasing clarity as each new layer of awareness takes me nearer to my core.

I empower myself and others in my life. I reach for the highest goals in whatever I do. I demonstrate my personal integrity by remaining true to myself and proving my authenticity in personal and professional situations. I appreciate my unique qualities as well as the uniqueness of others. My appreciation of myself opens up new opportunities for personal development. I am able to take full advantage of the new vistas I create for myself by my personal empowerment. I create a personal vision for myself. I see in me the potential that has previously been untapped. The limitless possibilities excite me!

* * *

I accept that change is possible for me in every aspect of my life as I acknowledge the value of realizing my personal power.

While I am in the process of change, I allow new energy to enter my life. I am able to be flexible in order to permit change to occur. As I break the thinking and behavior patterns that restrict me into a narrow focus, I am free to explore new and alternative ways of thinking and behaving. As I grow, I am able to explore the boundaries of who I am and who I can be. Being involved in the process of change can be a stabilizing force in my life. I am aware of the core of my personality which will remain true to itself and be the calming directing force in the course of changing the patterns which inhibit my growth. I look foward to the outcome as I relish my freedom to choose.

*　　*　　*

By stretching my imagination, I create new possibilities in life.

Food has been replaced as the center of my life. Now I am able to focus my attention on my whole being. I no longer judge my emotional reaction to people or events by the amount of food I eat or restrict in any particular day. I review each day and look at my personal relationships and interactions — how I asserted myself and how I affirmed my self-worth. I allow for situations which are less than ideal. My barometer or measure of success is my ability to nurture myself and ask for support. I accept all my efforts to grow as being valuable.

*　　*　　*

As I focus my attention on my entire being, I measure my growth by my ability to nourish myself.

I attract growth and gainful situations in my life as I release myself from the worries and fears of the past. I pass through the invisible curtain of light which allows me to explore new territories in a step-by-step fashion. I trust my ability to pick and choose information that will help me in my process of change. I trust my body to choose foods that are healthy for me. As I respect every aspect of my being, I bring forth the more positive qualities of my personality. I notice that I like myself and enjoy my own company. As if by magic, my life is falling into place.

* * *

I am initiating a new way of life as I free myself from the fears of the past.

The power of my commitment to health
and well-being will carry me through this
day. When I feel the need to engage in any
compulsive activity, whether it is excessive
exercise, a binge cycle or restricting food, I
commit to making a choice that will lift me
to a new awareness of myself. I focus on my
long-term goal of peace and health. I am no
longer willing to accept self-sabotage, which
was my pattern of yesterday. Today I renew
my commitment to growth and willingly
welcome the experiences which challenge
my emotional investment in life. Knowing
that I will reach out for support in rough
times reassures me in accepting the challenges that lie before me.

*   *   *

*I commit myself to choosing the experience
rather than imposing an external block to shut
it out.*

I generate positive energy and allow positive people in my life, motivating myself and supporting my growth. I shed the old patterns of my life and the maladaptive patterns of my family as I forge ahead with a sense of confidence in my future. Today is the beginning of my commitment to my own future without being weighed down by the millstone of the past. Looking to this day as a new beginning, I am grateful for the lessons I have learned. I am able to tap my vitality. I assert myself as I reach for new heights in my ability to care for my needs. My eating patterns become less important as I focus my attention on engaging in life to the fullest. I accept myself and respect my unique process of growth.

* * *

I release the patterns from my past as I am able to acknowledge the value of the lessons I have learned.

Expressing my feelings gives me a sense of assurance. I experience pleasure on a deep emotional level which revitalizes my spirit. I feel free of the chains of pent-up anger. Giving myself permission first to feel and then to express what I experience affirms my self-esteem. My self-assurance and sense of pleasure is communicated to others by the feeling of confidence that radiates from within and expresses itself through my body. My internal experience of self-confidence matches my external expression, leading to a feeling of wholeness. Developing my inner resources has given me the emotional luxury of integration.

*   *   *

I feel confident and self-assured as my level of feelings revitalizes me from within.

I am able to nurture myself in equal proportion to what I give others. I recognize the signals in my body which let me know when I need my own nurturing attention. I no longer reach for food or restrict food as a response to this need. I have the newfound ability to soothe myself. I relish my ability to balance my needs and to discern the natural response to satisfy these needs. As I love myself in a refreshing, life-giving way, I am able to reparent the child within me. I am fully aware of myself and rejoice at the opportunity to give myself what I need. My life is fuller with the newfound awareness of my ability to take care of my needs.

*   *   *

I have the resources to balance my needs against that of others and call forth responses to satisfy them.

I am consciously changing my relationship with my body. Each day I mentally embrace each body part and reinforce the positive aspects. By doing this, I actively work on accepting myself in a systematic way. I enjoy my body, its curves and the style of my movements. I feel comfortable in my body. Each day I wake up visualizing how I plan to nurture my body without relying on food. I take a leisurely walk, a bubble bath or a refreshing ride in my car with the breeze blowing through my hair. I feel I can freely participate in life. I create the body image that I wish to express from the inside. My sense of my body is integrated with who I am.

* * *

As I become more and more comfortable with myself, my body reflects the changes taking place from within.

Play and laughter, the universal language, will be my goal today. I look forward to experiencing this day with a childlike joy. I seek out someone to play with or my own better self to experience my inner joy. I anticipate the joy that accompanies a new awareness within me. I appreciate my ability to understand the information that is presented to me in this process of growth. I am eager to accept the process of change and make it a part of my daily life. Growth is exciting. I witness that which I manifest in my inner and outer reality. I am able to keep my faith in myself as I experience the freedom that comes with the renewal of the spirit.

* * *

I am in full possession of my sense of self and my level of joy manifests my new awareness.

Interrupting my old patterns around food is now second nature to me. I look forward to the day when I will no longer experience the need for sameness and ritual to feel secure. The feeling of security occurs within me as I stabilize my image of myself and interact from a place of assuredness and conviction. I gradually feel the process change in that direction and each day remind myself where I have come from and where I am going. I recognize the stages of growth and feel my center becoming stronger as I visualize my final goal. I accept myself as I am today so as to be able to accept the gradual changes that continue to occur.

*   *   *

I look at myself and where I am today and use this day as a frame of reference for change.

My love for myself encourages me to communicate with others. I communicate my wants, my needs, my hopes and my fears. I experience a feeling of safety within myself before I choose to express myself to others. As I feel safe with myself, I can trust others. I trust my body and its sensations. I appreciate my personal integrity in this discovery of my true self. I rework and ask for forgiveness first of myself for any past mistakes and then of others for any personal transgressions in the past. As I cleanse my own spirit, I am able to reach out to others from a clear centered perspective. As I look within and experience a renewal, I feel my self-respect being further anchored in my awareness.

*   *   *

As I honestly relate to myself, so I am able to express myself honestly to others.

I look at any anxiety I may feel today as a sign that I am willing to initiate a new level of exploration. Rather than see it as a signal that needs to be quieted with food or a compulsion, I choose to consider the experience as the beginning of yet another level of feeling. Each time I reach the pinnacle of my life, I am willing to accept the challenge of a new level of growth. Each time I do, I am enriched by my own resources which at times seem boundless. I only accept the challenge of exploration when I feel complete at the previous level of change. I trust my inner sense of timing and harmony.

*　　　*　　　*

Today I accept my anxiety as a healthy sign that I am ready to move on to a new level of growth.

I am flexible and creative in my thinking. I am able to handle situations in my day-to-day life with a sense of hope and enthusiasm. I trust my ability to take care of myself. I appreciate my sensitivity towards others. I am able to look out for the interests of everyone concerned in a situation. I feel a sense of wholeness when all the people involved experience satisfaction. I accept my limits in all situations while being sensitive to the needs of others. I am aware of myself at all times and choose to maintain my sense of personal integrity. My boundaries are clear as I operate from a place of internal satisfaction.

*   *   *

I have developed the ability to be sensitive to others and their interests while taking care of myself.

I experience a healing light filter through every aspect of my being. I attract the light to heal my spirit so that I may experience life on a higher level. I absorb the amount of light each day which enhances my involvement with myself and others. I feel comfortable alone and in crowds. My presentation is the same with all people I meet. My consistency gives me the foundation to grow and continue to transform myself to the best of my ability. I am stimulated by the light within me. I am the light of my life.

*   *   *

As I bring the light down into the darkness of my layers of compulsion, I free another part of myself and move up in the process of healing.

Living in the present has opened my eyes to a new way of being. I find my spontaneity refreshing as do others in my life. I enjoy my own company and am able to feel rewarded with an appreciation of myself. As I become more and more satisfied with myself, I radiate a level of peace that regenerates my spirit. My commitment to growth comes from deep within me rather than from external reasons to change my weight and shape. Life has taken on a richness as I foster my growth on every level. Food and weight are not issues as I encourage nurturing experiences for my whole self. I am free to be who I am in each and every moment.

*   *   *

Superficial changes no longer have a place in my quest for contentment with myself.

At some point in my recovery process, I have hit bottom. I have established a new and different format for my life. I have set goals based on my needs, my wants and my plans for the future. I have put myself, with my healthy long-term interests first rather than giving myself food in the short run. I have allowed myself to express my true self. I have come out of my cocoon, ready to fly but this time I have one foot firmly planted in the present with an eye towards my future goal. I put forth my energy into the world through my loved ones and through my work. I manifest my true spirit in my love for myself and for others. I value myself.

*   *   *

My rootedness in the present gives me a sense of self that I have previously been unwilling to acknowledge.

I function as my own inner parent to my vulnerable child. I am the nurturing loving parent who is aware of and responsive to my own needs. I choose to listen to my innermost thoughts. I answer the depth of my needs without judgment or fear. I am learning to anticipate my wants and needs and am now able to provide the support and motivation in getting those needs met, just as a loving parent would. Life is getting smoother as I channel my resources to the fundamental level of listening to the Higher Power in helping myself in my day-to-day life. I deserve to be listened to. I begin each day by checking in with myself as I wake up. I love myself.

*   *   *

As parent to my inner child, it is my privilege to protect the child and respond to the child's needs.

Befriending my body leads to positive respect for my sexuality. When I feel fat, I feel unaccepted. When I feel thin, I expect that I will be suddenly transformed and accepted. I release the old standards for my body as I discard society's demands for perfection. I establish my own standards for my body by looking at my personal heritage and by reclaiming my values for my life as a whole. I release the illusions of my life being *fixed* by slimness. I enhance my already positive attitudes about my body by focusing on my positive qualities — both internal and external — which create my concept of myself as a whole, healthy loving being.

* * *

I embrace my own healthy, innate sexual nature that corresponds to my general feelings about life and intimacy.

Filling myself with food keeps me from exploring my inner self. Food fills spaces I am fearful of going into. I am now courageous and ready to explore every aspect of myself. I give myself permission to eat so that I may be able to nurture my inner needs. Food has been a convenient way to hide my personal expression of my needs and feelings. I am pleased with my decision to experience my feelings directly without the defense of food. I acknowledge my humanity by expressing myself. I can accept care and nurturance from others in my environment. Indeed, the healthy part of me seeks out those who can be supportive of my needs which I express with the confidence that they can be met.

*   *   *

I encourage myself to go to the limits of my emotional life because only then will I be able to express my true self.

In the past my life was organized around the structure of the diet. Today I organize it around my feelings and true needs. I welcome the hunger cues and ask myself what would please me just as I would ask guests in my home what their wants and needs are. I enjoy the challenge of satisfying my hunger with food I enjoy. When I feel satiated I stop eating and allow the food inside to soothe me. I remind myself that I can eat more if I continue to feel hungry. On those days when I may feel hungry all day, I wait five minutes before I eat in order to experience any other feelings I have that may resemble hunger. I allow them to come through me, knowing that I can deal with such feelings and memories.

* * * *

I only eat in response to physiological hunger.

As I wake this morning I bear in mind that it is a new day with new choices in front of me. I may have backslid yesterday and binged but I do not have to repeat this behavior today. I am not stuck in the cycle of binging and restricting but am free to make new and different choices for myself today. Just because I took a step backward yesterday does not mean I cannot take a step forward today. I forgive myself for previous bad decisions, gently, as if I were a little child, and then look foward to the coming day with anticipation, knowing that with the help of the Higher Power I can continue to grow in my recovery.

*   *   *

As I forgive myself, I free myself to realize my full potential in the world today.

I awake today with a sense of adventure. I approach my recovery from compulsive eating as a journey into my inner core, my true self. My life has somehow led me to this point in my recovery. I now willingly explore the issues that are central to my eating behavior, whether I restrict or binge. I am aware that although my environment has been an influence in my compulsive eating, I am the only one who can truly help me recover. I embrace this opportunity for independence. I enjoy the feeling of freedom when I can eat according to my physical cues. I go with the flow of my internal cues and express my feelings.

*   *   *

I invest my energy in changing myself rather than in changing the environment or changing others.

The glamorous fantasy of thinness is no longer a motivating factor in my life. My goal during recovery is the resolution of the past so that I may live in the present. Life moves along at a lighter pace these days as I love myself and motivate myself to reach the limits of my capacity. The feeling of lightness comes from within. As I have released the burden of the expectations of perfection in my actions as well as in my body image, I am acutely aware of the emotional baggage that has been removed. I am no longer obsessed by weight and food. Food has become pleasurable to me again.

*   *   *

I put my real self in my fantasies as I visualize myself in action — assertive, expressive, sensitive and content with the body I have.

I accept my natural body type. I go with the flow of life, beginning with my genetic makeup. I work with the positive points of my body and enhance these aspects. I minimize rather than accentuate what I consider to be my weak body points. I focus on the positive body parts as I consider my choice of clothes for today. I am aware that what I say to myself about my body creates feelings about my self-worth. I actively express my feelings and thoughts about my body. Reaffirming the positive enhances my self-image. I am my own best friend as I support my positive efforts during recovery.

*   *   *

I highlight the positive aspects of my body in dress, movement and feelings as I support my efforts in recovery.

Manipulating my body weight is a false way to achieve a sense of control. I am learning that true control comes from a balance between inner feelings and thoughts and my outward behavior. When I express my feelings, whether positive or negative, I feel balance returning to my life. I experience a sense of order coming from within myself, rather than from the external structure of a diet or a food ritual. This inner peace gives me the opportunity to explore my options in life. I feel safe within as I befriend myself. I participate in life as I experience the present from a sense of self-possession and autonomy.

* * *

As I increase my awareness of myself and learn true control, I am ready to approach my body as a place where I safely live.

I challenge myself to reach a new level in my recovery. I explore long-term and short-term goals in life as I put my priorities in order. Now that weight is not the foremost issue in my life, I am able to focus on living. I find that releasing my fears about my body and weight has freed me from the past and from concern about the future. Now, today is the most important period in my life. I am able to direct my energy to tangible issues rather than live in the fantasy of a thin body as the ultimate goal. I measure my success with the depth of feeling I am able to achieve and experience my life from moment to moment.

* * *

Today is the beginning of my commitment to my own future without the excess baggage of the past or fantasies of the future.

Establishing my own boundaries, my own limits in each area of my life, helps me in relinquishing compulsive behavior. I continue to pull energy into my center to focus awareness on my body. I make clear choices when I am free to focus on the purpose of my behavior. Getting lost in compulsive activity happens when I choose to remain unaware of the feelings which precipitate each event. I give myself permission to experience the sensations that occur within my body. I feel that life is going to be within my control: I am never given more than I can handle at any one time in life. Purposeful behavior is inherently more satisfying to me than succumbing to impulse or engaging in compulsive activity.

* * *

Staying with my natural energy helps me to regulate my impulses.

Finding my center is comforting when everything around me appears chaotic. I become my own focal point. I focus on the center line in my body which is a source of renewal and strength. I fill my sense of center with comforting thoughts, words, images, colors and feelings. I view this center line as a column of light. The light recharges my spirit and is a source of continual energy which flows gently through my whole body. Focusing on my center helps me to reduce my desire for food which previously filled the only sense of center I knew. Now, living in the light encourages me to experience the presence of the Higher Power which directs me towards health and recovery.

*　　*　　*

I am recharged spiritually as I focus on my center and allow the light to energize me.

Reflecting on the wonders of nature brings me back to the purpose of life. It makes me fully comprehend growth and change. I recognize the ebb and flow of all life that comforts me in times of need. I focus on the dawn of each day as a new experience, a new opportunity for growth and choice. Reflecting on nature helps me to consider my part in the scheme of life and the path that is being illuminated by my trust in the Higher Power. I commit myself to this day and to my ability to change one small part of my relationship with food. Nurturing my changes helps me to experience my unconditional positive regard for myself. I am grateful for the opportunity to bring about change in my life today which can rekindle my hope for success.

*   *   *

I reflect on nature to understand my part in life.

Affirming my authenticity in the world requires no action on my part. It is a simple state of being. It is the acceptance of myself with all my limitations and all my strengths. I simply accept my humanity. I am aware that I do not have to accomplish anything in order to establish my self-worth. My self-worth comes from *being* myself, rather than *doing* something in the world. In the quiet and peace of dawn or dusk, I am myself, at peace with my emotions, my history, my future and yet more important, being with myself is self-acceptance in the present moment. Affirming myself brings joy to me and others in my life.

* * *

I am open to receiving the gift of myself at the beginning of each new day as I affirm my being.

216

I am naturally attracted towards health, whether that be physical, emotional or spiritual health. Achieving health is a gentle process of going with the body rather than an exhaustive process of fighting the body's natural tendencies. As I become more and more comfortable with myself, my body reflects these changes coming from within. I befriend my body as I also befriend my emotional and spiritual aspects. I am an individual who has been created to seek and find happiness. I am in possession of myself. I acknowledge my unique goodness, my unique qualities, including my strengths and weaknesses. I appreciate myself and feel the joy that comes with true self-acknowledgment.

*   *   *

I focus my energies on achieving health.

My sense of self is separate from my actions and deeds. I am able to acknowledge my true goodness and worth without having to perform for others. I attract into my environment people who are also able to affirm my sense of self. My giving to others comes from my feeling of completeness and a desire to share myself with them. I am free to give. I go through the day affirming my sense of self without having to depend on the approval of others. My self-esteem is an internal positive self-regard that becomes more stable every day I value myself. I am grateful for this new found sense of self that increases with my self-affirmation.

* * *

My goodness manifests itself in my presence and in my actions as I choose to express my sense of self.

Through the process of self-affirmation, I am able to know myself. I accept myself unconditionally on an emotional level as well as on an intellectual level. I give love to myself without contingencies, without promises about my body size and weight, regardless of my past. I accept myself fully and without restraint. I reveal myself to others as I choose to acknowledge that my empowerment comes from my affirming myself. I know that the source of my strength lies within me and in my connection to the Higher Power. I empower myself as I am able to inspire others to live to the fullest with the gentleness and ease of self-acceptance.

*   *   *

I inspire others just by being myself and by my ability to accept them and myself unconditionally.

My innate sense of self-worth helps me in aspiring to expand my involvement in life. I demonstrate to others my own sense of self by affirming and acknowledging the essence of their being. I am able to give them what I have now received from myself and other loving people in my life. I give of myself generously as my needs are met and I feel validated. My sense of self encourages me to risk in some areas of my life and to pull myself back when I become over involved with others to the detriment of my own personal growth. I honor my dignity and self-worth and demonstrate this in all of my actions which are a reflection of myself.

*   *   *

My gifts now are more meaningful since I can truly let go of my attachment.

I am learning to turn my anger into action. Whereas food served as a way to stuff that very powerful feeling, now I am identifying the feeling of anger and expressing it. I own my anger and feel the need to express it in direct ways. I feel the energy holding back the feeling, yet I push past the fear and express it. I find that the results are positive: My desire to eat is diminished, my feelings have been expressed and I have taken the risk of supporting my feelings productively. I love becoming actualized. I thank the Higher Power for my strength to engage in meaningful interaction.

*   *   *

I support my feelings today by expressing my anger and turning it into meaningful action.

I am active, not reactive to others or situations. I value my ability to be a friend but I allow others the time and space to solve their own problems and handle their own pain. I respect their individuality as well as my own autonomy. My primary focus is on helping myself at this time. I am discovering that the better I treat myself, the better friend I can be to others. I give support and also ask for support. I am connected to others in a healthy way. My energy is recharged by giving to others from a place of safety within myself. I separate my actions from my self-worth. Learning to change my behavior and my relationships with others is a self-loving process.

*   *   *

I know my areas of responsibility and am careful not to take on more than I can actually handle.

I am aware of a vague and yet pervasive anxiety at the edge of my consciousness as I either move towards or away from food. I am beginning to witness the likeness of abundance and deprivation, the either/or nature of the situation. I approach the feelings of apprehension around food as a challenge. As I go deeper into those thoughts and feelings, I find that food plays no actual role at all, but has merely been a symbol for me, one that I could control. The feelings that I couldn't or shouldn't attach myself to anything or anyone continually externalized my fears and led me away from my center. I now release my use of food as a cover for my anxious feelings.

*   *   *

I am learning to utilize my anxiety to be the cue for a deeper search that requires time, patience and self-soothing.

Learning about my family history helps me to put my life into perspective. I clarify who I am and the patterns I have repeated. I embrace my power to change my relationship with the family and friends I have now. I am able to interact with others from the personal perspective of my family patterns. I identify with and learn from others in my past while allowing myself the separateness that comes with embracing my selfhood.

* * *

I open myself up to the self-discovery that comes from reviewing my family history.

I embrace the concept of possibility. Only when I can leave behind my preconceived notions of the way life "should be" can I accept the concept of change and trust in my ability to fulfill myself. Life is available for me to explore. I create my own reality. I affirm my abilities. I give myself permission to develop my potential. I take one step at a time towards my long-term goals. I include my ability to overcome compulsive eating in the long-range plans for my life. My eating or desire to eat represents my zest for life. I explore my talents with the same enthusiasm.

* * *

Today I drop my conditioned ideas of what life should be and decide to explore its many hidden possibilities.

I experience increasing wonder as I truly befriend myself. My ability to give to myself and to listen to the wants and needs of my body fills me with joy. I feel satisfied after each meal. I enjoy pleasing my body, mind and spirit as I seek nourishment for each aspect of myself. I can now decide which challenges I want to undertake at this point in my recovery. I make room for myself to grow in each area as I resolve old issues and make way for new material to surface. I peel away the layers of my life to search deeper and deeper for the truth that lies within me. My Higher Power leads the way to permanent change and recovery.

*   *   *

My goals for myself are realistic in that I take each day and each issue as it comes.

I challenge my perfectionist thoughts about my performance and self-worth. I am realistic about my expectations of myself. I am pleased that I can let go of my all-or-nothing thinking. I accept my efforts as the best I can do today. Accepting my limitations in all areas of my life makes each day a little easier. I accept my humanity and understand that dichotomies like black and white, good and bad keep me stuck in the rut of dissatis-faction and rigidity. I no longer have to be perfect to win others' approval as well as my own. How freeing it is to relax the rigid standards which actually prevented my growth! I am patient with myself as I con-front my own rigid thinking.

*   *   *

I am growing more realistic and allow for mistakes as I release my perfectionist way of life.

I surround myself with my support system when I wish to binge. I recognize that withdrawal, isolation and subsequent loneliness are triggers for binging. I utilize my support system in a healthy life-promoting way. I appreciate myself and am able to accept the caring offered to me, knowing that I am worthy of being loved. I no longer expect myself to handle everything alone. I have the ability to attract healthy supportive people into my life. I can be a friend to others as well as to myself. My inner life is enriched by my true friends. I feel the warmth and glow in an honest exchange between two friends. I bask in my friends' love as I move along the path of recovery.

* * *

I am free to ask for support if I am afraid of resorting to food.

I actively ward off the desire to binge by eating enough each day. I choose my food with care. I grade my hunger and my level of fullness at each meal or snack I eat. I observe the warning signals of being too hungry by eating a small portion before the meal is fixed. I trust my body to help me regulate my food intake. When I feel that I may not be able to trust my body, I acknowledge that feeling also. I ask for support when I am unsure of my ability to be prudent around food. I create a supportive environment in response to my internal needs as I release my need to be in control at all times. This gives me the freedom to grow and change.

* * *

I enjoy eating now that I am able to stop when I feel full.

My goal is possible: I can release myself from the habit of compulsive eating. My diet is healthy while still allowing me the foods I enjoy. I make sure that the quantities I eat are limited. I ward off binge episodes with a healthy balance of exercise, relaxation, visualizations of my best self and judicious quantities of food. I am a success story. My life has been a long journey to get to the place I have reached today. Each day, though, I strive for continued success. I have put the wheels in motion and reap the benefits of my commitment to growth.

*   *   *

I challenge myself to reach new heights of awareness, knowing that the changes come now in natural progression.

Looking at my eating habits over the past several years, I can see that my dieting has shortchanged me emotionally. By allowing my diet to be ruled by some arbitrary new food plan or belief system, I have deprived myself of the opportunity to respond to my natural instincts about my nourishment. I have now come to embrace the idea that my body, if allowed to, will accurately respond to my signals for food and nourishment. I accept the fact that my body type was determined at birth. I encourage myself to accept my body and my natural need for food. I enjoy being spontaneous in my choice of foods. Each meal and snack is a joyous event as I release the old attitudes and embrace the way of life that is natural and healthy for me.

*   *   *

I substitute nourishment for arbitrary food plans.

Dieting is a life-control issue as well as a body/food-control dilemma. I release control over my body by allowing myself to respond to internal cues and by feeding myself emotionally with support, love and nurturance. I enjoy my right to eat when I am hungry and stop when I am full. Being perfect on the outside now symbolizes chaos on the inside. I am now focusing my energies inward towards my emotional and spiritual well-being. I release the comparison of myself to models who bear no resemblance to my ancestry. I accept my heritage and the power I have inherited. I embrace life with a more spontaneous attitude.

*   *   *

I am able to distance myself from the old images of perfection and understand their futility.

The scales are no longer the barometer of my happiness or self-esteem. I have long since discarded my scales and traded them for self-love and self-respect as the measure. I check into my "love bank" when the external world gets too hectic for me. I shore myself up emotionally each day by reminding myself of my own self-love. I also look to others in my life who affirm my self-worth. I view all my pleasures as radiating from within me to my external world. It is safe to continue to check into my self-love for emotional reassurance. I release any criticism that I may have left over from the past by validating myself in the present with love and caring. I value myself.

*   *   *

Using internal monitors for affirming myself has kept my life on an even keel.

The interplay between my body and my environment is always in a state of flux. I express my feelings as well as the suppression of my feelings through my body. Dispensing with dieting has encouraged me to look at my body realistically and to accept my natural body type. As I allow myself to eat, I encourage myself to accept my feelings and to express them in a supportive environment. I enjoy the health that food gives my body and the vitality I feel when I eat what my body selects. I accept my power to choose attitudes and beliefs which enhance my life. I can now choose how others' attitudes will affect my life as well. I am overcoming yet one more hurdle in the process of recovery.

*   *   *

I replace the passive need for food with my new expression of feelings, making my needs known.

I choose the people in my environment who affirm my inner goodness. By their support, I am able to have my sense of self acknowledged. This gives me the strength to continue to grow. Change is a slow process, yet each day that I am able to affirm myself, I reinforce my commitment to the process with renewed fervor. I allow myself to grow at a rate that is comfortable for me. I challenge myself to move forward, yet I am able to remain still at times when no action is required. I am open to the changes that occur at subtle levels.

*   *   *

I look to the changes in nature and the slow process of growth to remind myself not to rush the process but to accept myself as I am today.

The quest for perfection limits my choices in life and sets me up to feel inadequate about my humanity. I change the old standards for my life by relaxing my expectations daily. I am no longer in quest of the perfect body but make an effort for a healthy body. I no longer expect perfect performance but a moderate approach to achievement in all areas of my life. I nourish my opportunities for growth without putting undue pressure on myself. I support my growth processes by acknowledging that I am learning about myself from the inside out as I reduce my expectations. I am learning and living as I change.

*   *   *

I release the old expectations and take each day as it comes.

I am learning to promise myself and others less than I may actually deliver. I allow myself the freedom to do more when the time comes yet I am actively changing my approach to overcommitment. This immediately reduces the stress in my life. As I breathe more freely and let the idea sink into my psyche, I am able to accept the space which I have just given myself. Releasing excessive expectations has a direct result on my compulsive eating. I no longer feel I have to nourish myself with food since I no longer give myself and my time away. Releasing my hold on myself and others encourages me to explore the freedom I am entitled to.

*   *   *

I choose my commitments carefully and give of myself as I wish.

I acknowledge my need to continue with the process of growing and affirming myself. I embrace the opportunity to put my plans for growth into action. I accept the up-and-down process of change and dwell only on the positive aspects while I learn from the past. I look at my shortcomings with the realism of an adult rather than the demanding attitude of a child. I change what is possible for me to change and accept what is impossible to change. I accept the body I have with all its desires and needs. I am willing and able to meet those needs and desires when appropriate. I thank the Higher Power for the gifts I have and see my shortcomings as lessons to be learned.

* * *

I accept my humanity at times of change and know that perfection is an unrealistic goal.

My body speaks to me when I am hungry, when I accept fullness and when I acknowledge my inner instinctual voice. My body has a natural propensity towards health. Acknowledging my body's messages is a gift to myself. I discern the different messages that my body gives as I am challenged by my own diversity. I approach life with a feeling of safety as I rely on my body's signals. Eating when I feel hungry is the first action I can take to reinforce the positive messages of my body. Trusting my body is my gift to myself. The miracle of life lies in the cellular messages that created life.

*   *   *

I feel safe in life as I continue to become aware of my body's subtle language and heed its messages.

I remove the word fat from my vocabulary. I affirm my body by accepting the size I am today. I choose to release any label with regard to my body size. I experience the feeling of my body as I promote change. I encourage myself to take care of my body by giving it the foods I find pleasing and by increasing my physical activity. I give my body time to rest when I am sleepy or stressed. I put food in the proper perspective when I consider my body's true needs. I think of it as caring for an infant and the many needs that arise in the course of a day. My body has the same needs. I value myself as I learn to meet my various needs.

* * *

I am the parent to my body.

As I accept the natural rhythm of my body, I am able to feed myself and further my new body awareness. I take cues from my body to eat when I am hungry and stop when I am full. I am learning to differentiate the various cues my body gives. I recognize that food is one of my needs and I eat satisfying meals in response to that need. My movement style is also unique to me and I feel a certain joy of movement as I simply walk down the street. I focus on the internal messages of my body rather than on external appearance as I feel positive energy flow through my body. I take pleasure in the way my body feels as I move through the day.

*   *   *

I notice my movement style and encourage myself to express my personal rhythm to others.

241

I am able to actively choose what is happening in my life. My trust in myself and my respect for my needs enable me to make choices that are in my best interest. Just as I am learning to recognize physical hunger and rewarding this newfound awareness with an appropriate choice of food, I am acknowledging the needs in every aspect of my life. My emotional and physical needs are my cues and my choices are my responses. I no longer feel that I have to please others before I please myself. I remain aware of and respond to other people's needs. However, I am active in choosing my response to them. I feel the freedom and lightness which accompanies this choosing.

*   *   *

As I honor my physical and emotional cues, I become free to choose my responses to others' needs.

As I look at my body, I am aware of the external changes that reflect the deeper internal transformation. I am empowered by the reflection I see before me. I suspend all judgment as I observe myself in the mirror. I accept myself as I am at this moment. I am the affirming self that encourages myself to continue to grow and change on my path to self-actualization. I encourage the beauty within me to blossom and I manifest this through my personal expression. I am more than my accomplishments. I love myself for being who I am today and for who I have always been. I reflect the love I feel from the Higher Power.

* * *

I enjoy the feeling of peace as I quiet the judge and jury within me.

I am victorious in my struggle with food. I am grateful for the growth opportunities my compulsive behavior has provided me. I would not be at this level of growth were it not for my ability to overcome my obsession with food and weight. I live in peace in my body as I am able to accept my shape and weight as they are now. Food does not have the hold over me it once did. I acknowledge my need for food, yet when I am in a stressful situation, I no longer turn to it as an answer to my emotional needs. Food tastes especially good to me now when I am hungry as I have learned to gauge my appetite and respond to my body's needs.

*   *   *

The world looks brighter to me today as I review my past and anticipate my continued success in my growth.

Love is the bond between me and others. I express my gratitude to others by showing my love. Sharing love emphasizes my caring for myself and others. True love is reflected in all that I do. The giving that comes from my heart is different from the feeling of having to give; true sharing involves my being. The more I grow and develop self-love, the more I am able to give to others. I express my appreciation to those who have expressed their love for me by giving love in return. I also share love with those who are not able to share it with me. I seek the Higher Goodness in my interaction with others.

*   *   *

I am thoughtful in loving myself as only then can I be thoughtful in loving others.

My life is dynamic. It is a source of experience and growth. I approach each day with a feeling of adventure. I choose what I want to become involved with and what is not in my best interest. I establish direction in my life each day as I awake. I have a goal in mind and I work towards this goal, being careful to allow flexibility for living each day. Each day I am aware of being filled with the presence of the Higher Power. This is the inner source of my dynamic existence. Each small action I perform is filled with the wondrous presence of that which is greater than I. I work for the better good in all I do. I praise my participation in life by making the world a better place for everyone to live.

*   *   *

I am the catalyst for the chemistry of my life.

In stressing the positive aspects of my life, I continually strive to maximize my potential. When I see life in a positive way, the light changes as if I have turned on an electric lamp. I am illuminating the possibilities for change. Life is not meant to be stagnant. Longing for yesterday forces me to live in the past. Hoping for a miraculous change — whether it is a perfect weight, body, mate or job offer — keeps me fixed on an illusive future. Living in the present and being content with the body and the life I have created thus far allows me to be in charge of today and of the tomorrows that manifest my true potential. I am empowered by my freedom to choose.

*   *   *

I choose to see the struggles as a means for growth.

Making positive growth-producing changes in my life may mean allowing some people to go. While relationship patterns may not always be pleasant or healthy, they are the known. What is known becomes comfortable. Giving up the comfortable for the unknown usually produces fear. However, letting someone go may be the only way to make room for a better individual to come into my life. I give each person the benefit of the doubt and the opportunity to grow and change prior to making any decision about releasing him or her from my life. Opening up relationships and allowing the light of awareness to shine through will encourage each person to seek the strength within the self. It gives both parties the opportunity to see life through the window of their soul.

*   *   *

I release unhealthy relationships for positive change.

248

My life is an affirmation of trust and courage. I take my life beyond struggles as I release judgments about my life. My battle with food, whether it is restricting or binging, is symbolic of how I coped with life when it was difficult for me. I choose today to release my negative opinions about food, my body and my self-worth. I embrace my ability to free my life of struggle and conflict. I am free of the past as I move into today with the hope of a positive sense of self. My life has provided me with challenges which strengthen my commitment to change. I call upon the Higher Power to reinforce my courage and silence my self-doubt.

*   *   *

I evoke my strength as a survivor to continually motivate myself as I grow in knowledge and peace.

I approach this day with a commitment to flexibility. I release my preconceived notions about control and my struggle with food. I acknowledge my former need to control my external world in order to have a feeling of inner control. My goal for today is to get in touch with my feelings and to respond to them as I become aware of each feeling. I am flexible with food and mealtimes. I listen to my internal hunger cues rather than to the lunch bell. I eat foods that are appealing to me. I love and respect my body as I respect my need for food. My appetite is appropriate for my body type. My bodily wants work in unison with my body's needs.

*   *   *

I am more flexible in my attitude to life as I move with ease to satisfy my wants and needs.

My body has a memory. I acknowledge my body's ability to remember past events. I listen to the cues and allow the thoughts to flow through my mind as my body reacts to present stimuli and past events. I respect my body's ability to respond on a physical level. I love the feeling of my body moving through space. I focus my attention on the process of moving and breathing. The process is enhanced by my awareness of my body. I appreciate the qualities of my movement which has a language of its own. The complexity of my movements reflects my uniqueness. I honor my movement style as I flow through space with assurance and ease.

*   *   *

I interact with my environment through my senses and through movement.

My style of movement is a metaphor for my personal growth. I move my body in a way that reflects my positive hopeful sense of life. I keep a photographic or some other descriptive log of the experience of my body as I transform my attitude from body-loathing to body-loving. The changes are subtle as I reacquaint myself with my body. I befriend my body as I fully participate in daily life. I can change. I can grow in beauty and self-love. All options for growth and change are presented to me every day. Each experience I have is an opportunity to move forward. My personal development is enriched by the people in my life. I accept each phase of my life's cycle and make realistic goals at the appropriate time. Self-improvement include all areas of my life.

*   *   *

I stress the positive aspects of my body and personality.

There are consequences of changing my behavior that I willingly and actively pursue. When I take risks, for example, in becoming assertive, entering a new social situation or finding a job that will challenge my talents, I accept the fears that accompany these experiences, for only in those moments will I find growth. I am willing to risk not getting everything I want. By staying in the present and not relying on being saved by one particular success, I do not set myself up for extreme disappointment. I had previously chosen to stay the same because, on some level, I felt comfortable with behaviors without risk, no matter what the feelings of failure or guilt that followed the actions connected with my struggles with food. Now I am willing to accept fear and risk on a step-by-step basis.

* * *

I allow myself a level that is appropriate for me on this particular day.

When food helped to protect me from feeling, my thoughts were always on food. Now I am free to choose where I direct my thinking. I choose to think of food only when I am hungry or when I am planning a meal. I easily shift my thoughts to subjects more fulfilling than food and weight. Releasing my obsessions gives me the opportunity and freedom to act. I am aware that compulsive behavior is an activity rather than an action. I am action-oriented. Redirecting my energy allows me to choose the direction for my actions. Taking responsibility for my actions helps my growth. I am willing to accept the consequences of my actions and any positive feedback that come my way.

*   *   *

I choose to accept my actions as a reflection of my inner strength.

My spirit guides me. My faith in the Higher Power gives me peace. I am willing to participate in the flow of life. I move my body in such a way as to express my positive hopeful sense of self. I shift my focus to living life fully and participating in the present. I rely on my quest for wholeness that emanates from the healthy life-promoting part of myself. In the moments just before eating, I reflect on the spiritual aspect of my journey of discovery and imagine the emptiness I feel being lit with a glow from my center. I allow the light to fill me as it breaks down my resistance to eating or my inclination to binge.

*   *   *

I accept the peace that the connection with the Higher Power brings me.

I respect my sense of rhythm and timing. When it is time to act, I am assured of my ability to make decisions. When it is appropriate for me to wait, I am able to do so. There is a certain sense of relief in knowing that I am not always in charge. There is also a certain sense of fear that comes over me when I may feel as if I am not in control. I move into the fear, allowing myself to feel it without eating. I experience control of myself from within, which encourages me to be free. There is a softness to letting go that is different from being compliant. The playful child within me is allowed to come to the fore. I am flexible as I feel a sense of security within myself.

*   *   *

I feel safe going with the flow of life rather than attempting to chisel out my own rigid structure.

There is grace and beauty in my movements. I move with the flowing motions that express my true feelings. I explore the masculine/feminine side of myself as I free my body from the rigidity of self-contempt. My stiff exterior was merely a protective shield against the fear of becoming free-floating. My actions correspond with my appetite for food. The rigidity of diet was the only way to protect myself from my fear of overwhelming hunger. I accept my appetite as I learn that my flowing movements reflect my true feelings. I am able to be flexible in my choice of food as well.

* * *

I float free and easy as I remove the shields that protected me from my fears of deprivation.

Nourishing my body and my feelings is a process which involves time and energy. The first step is to listen to my body to decide if physical hunger, thirst or the need for sleep or relaxation is prominent in my hierarchy of needs. The next step is to listen to the automatic thoughts that may be creating feelings which either lead me to eat compulsively or to restrict food. Each need is specific and I direct my attention to the impulse to eat or restrict. Eating to suppress hurt, losses, anger or frustration is like sweeping dust under a rug — it is only a temporary measure. I visualize life without compulsively eating or restricting food as I work on this behavior.

*   *   *

The more I become aware of my own specific wants or needs, the more freely I am able to express myself.

I give myself permission to nurture myself. I take time out to fill my own needs in the middle of chaos, at lunch, during a break from work or school or after the children are asleep. This time is precious to me. The quantity of time is not as important as the quality of my giving. Working this into my daily routine is a gradual process. However, I notice that the more I give to myself in small ways regularly, the less need I have to eat compulsively or to restrict food. I identify needs which I previously ignored. I take the time to read something interesting or watch a movie or fix my hair in new and exciting ways. I nourish myself and take pleasure in my recovery.

*   *   *

I have come to rely on the little things in life I give to myself.

I am motivated to succeed. I reinforce this desire each and every day as I wake up. I am strengthened by my recent successes and challenged by new opportunities that arise. I learn more about myself in relation to food each day. I allow pictures to come into my mind as I focus on the day ahead. New rituals allow me to eat in response to hunger as I gradually become attuned to my physical and emotional needs. I release the shame about my body as I continually nurture myself. I release my fear of eating in front of others as I focus on *my* reaction to my nurturing rather than on what I imagine others are thinking about my eating. My gentleness with myself is the key to my success.

*   *   *

I gently remove myself from former patterns as I develop new rituals that insure my success.

The quality of my giving to others is a reflection of what I give to myself. I am able to give from a place of contentment and peace once I have satisfied my own needs. At times, I am aware that I cannot satisfy all my needs at the moment yet I make an effort to give to myself as a reminder that I am not deprived. I am fulfilled in life and revitalized by my ability to meet my own needs. I believe in myself and my self-worth. I respond to my own unique needs, knowing that they are different from what others may need at the time. I am aware that each need is different. My needs and wants are manageable. I am an exciting multifaceted individual.

*   *   *

I spend a little time on self-gratification to ease my need to eat or restrict food.

The process of recovery is about my taking charge of my own life. I no longer live the roles I accepted long ago. People in my life may have meant well, but I took the lessons of "should" too seriously for my own well-being. As I shed the old roles, I am able to carve out a new vitality for myself. I can be alive in my roles rather than routinely perform the tasks at hand. I am creating my own way of life and I begin by loving myself. I continually reinforce my love by acknowledging my zest for living. I am an expert in my own healing. It is in my hands to satisfy my needs and to ask for support when I need it. I nurture the seed of recovery as I witness my own blossoming.

*   *   *

I take charge of my life as I shed my old roles and create my own ways of living.

After so many diets, exercise programs and plans for reshaping the external forces in my life, I always ask myself what will make this attempt at recovery so different. The answer comes to me slowly and honestly — self-love. No one can love me if I do not first love myself. If I do not love myself, I will sabotage any potentially loving relationship. My dependency needs cannot be met by anyone else at this stage of my life. Growing up requires that I learn to love myself so that I can make decisions in my best interest. It begins with today. I will do something each day that reminds me of my goal of self-love. I separate loving myself from my behavior. My love for myself is unconditional

*   *   *

When I perform each small act of caring about my needs and wants, I am one step closer to my goal.

Following through with recovery is different from following a diet plan. Recovery is a way of life rather than an external event. Recovery comes from the inside and is manifested outward. There are no restrictions in recovery; only the requirement that I honestly meet each new day with a commitment to honor my process and accept myself as I am today. Each day is a new beginning. I accept my issues with food and understand that I do not have to give it up. I adjust myself to eating and enjoying food again during recovery. I enjoy tasting food as I eat slowly, savoring each bite. I prepare food that is appealing to me. Mealtime is an event to look forward to when I am hungry.

*   *   *

I feel free to satisfy myself now that I know I can meet my own needs for nurturance and love in recovery.

I release my judgments about my body which have been part of my compulsive behavior around food. My body has survived the mistreatment I have meted out. I accept my body as I break my compulsive habits. My body is a reflection of my attitudes to it; the more I honor and respect it, the more beautiful and spontaneous it becomes. Life is an opportunity for spontaneous expression. I no longer have to hold life back. I am able to fully express myself in every arena of my life. I am sensitive and aware in each situation as I continue to focus on my body and my feelings. I am free to anticipate and explore satisfying ways to express my feelings.

*   *   *

Now I am willing to acknowledge that there is more to life than mere survival.

Binging or restricting becomes unnecessary when I express my feelings. Remaining in touch with my body is the key to recovery. I eat when I feel hungry and stop when I feel full. I cry when I feel sad, smile and laugh when I feel happy, shout when I feel angry, question the cause when I am confused or frustrated and assert myself when my rights are being violated. I am an active participant in life. My eating does not speak for me any longer. I speak and act in my best behalf. As I continue to practice the skills of asserting myself, I am accepting myself. It is okay not to be perfect. In fact, when I err, I know that I am human. I appreciate my humanity.

*   *   *

I accept my humanity and the possibility of my making mistakes.

My body is a reflection of my internal emotional life. My image of my body underlies my emotional development. I see myself as the person with whom I feel safe. I may outwardly fight this notion, yet inwardly I know that a too fat or too thin body image is a protection against my greatest fears. It is comfortable for me to stay in the body-loathing rut when the rest of my life is chaotic. Blaming my body for my failures is a safe bet. As I grow in knowledge of and faith in myself, I release the body image distortion. I discard the microscopic fixations about perfection as well as the denial of my true size. I can mold the realistic image of myself as I appreciate the body I have, the person I am.

*   *   *

I begin the process of change with acceptance of the true image of my body.

My sense of timing is something I am continually refining. Learning to eat according to my body's timing is a skill I am continuing to assimilate. Learning to speak up for myself in appropriate situations is also a matter of timing. I can be more effective with the proper timing in my assertiveness. Sometimes I learn to sit back and watch rather than speak up. I react more spontaneously when I am in step with the flow of events. I know that I cannot force events to occur but by participating fully, I am able to be a part of life. I go with the flow of events as I appreciate my new-found sense of timing.

*   *   *

I am no longer just an observer nor am I the force behind every situation.

I strive to examine my own critical attitude towards myself and others, knowing that this developed from a painful situation in my past. Keeping the critic inside me alive hides my creativity and subdues my spirit. I actively take risks in challenging my own critical nature, whereas in the past, perhaps in childhood, I was not equipped to stand up to my original critic. I am now ready emotionally to risk my own criticism and my imagined criticism from others as I free my expressive childlike side from its hiding place within my body. I silence the negative critic who took away my spontaneity much too soon in life.

*   *   *

I allow the monitors on my free expression to drop away as I get in touch with my sensitivity.

I differentiate between judgment and being judgmental. Judgment is my healthy adult self making decisions based on reality and factual information which may make me act in a certain way. My being judgmental or critical towards myself keeps me locked into a pattern of negativity and deprivation. I embrace the positive aspects of healthy judgments, yet I release the critical or judgmental attitudes I may have towards my body, my views about food and my self-worth. I unlock my spiritual joyous nature which reinforces my growth. Moving into health renews my strength and courage.

*   *   *

I embrace each situation which stimulates me to release judgmental attitudes and opinions from the past.

I am bridging the gap between known and unknown parts of myself. As I struggle with compulsive eating patterns, I gradually uncover the reasons behind this behavior. I release the known patterns around food as I am willing to explore the depth of my feelings. Taking the focus away from food and my body size allows me to feel the feelings which have been covered up by my preoccupation with something outside myself. I encourage myself to become the risk-taker. Many times I chose safety when I chose to focus on diets, body size or exercise. I feel safer within myself now as I am willing to focus on my feelings and my memories.

*   *   *

I explore my personal potential as I plumb the depths of my spirit.

My personal potential is masked by my struggles with food and weight. I skillfully hide my talents when I am fearful of risking expression. This pattern of behavior has become habitual. It had an origin and prior to that I had other means of expressing and coping. I quiet the turmoil that fear has created as I get in touch with my true desires. I allow myself to gradually remove the armor of food and weight as I begin to heal. My feelings may seem quite young as I begin to express them. I know that I will go through all the stages of development I may have skipped. It will take only a short time since now I am open to the experience of change and growth.

*   *   *

I have the potential to develop new patterns to replace habits that no longer benefit my experience.

Listening to my body is a natural, effective means of maintaining my healthy weight. I find that when I acknowledge my body cues and eat the foods I really want, I eat less than when I deprive myself and stay on a rigid diet. I deserve the best life has to offer. My body inherently knows this and now I am acknowledging this fact. My body does indeed know best. All those years of deprivation and dieting have not produced the desired results. I achieve my natural weight with nature's foods and nature's tools. The future holds promise as I acknowledge my body's wisdom.

*   *   *

I now listen to my body for what I want to eat and how much.

Challenging myself to reach my personal potential encourages me to explore my true gifts. To become my best self, I willingly test the limits of my capacities. Striving to be my best self requires soul-searching and perhaps some changing. This may require that I let go of situations in which I have control and in which there is little risk so that I have the space and time to develop capacities that stretch me to the limits of my abilities. I have the faith in myself and my personal potential to warrant a calculated risk. I know this may take time and effort on my part. I am willing to explore my potential so that I become the best I can be.

* * *

I must do what I enjoy in order to be my best self.

Food is my friend. It gives me the nutrition and strength I need to live a healthy, happy life. I respect the limits of food. While it provides me with the health I require physically, food also satisfies my sense of taste. I am learning to enjoy eating again. I remove the compulsive habits and rituals around food which previously gave me a feeling of safety. I am free from my attachment to food and therefore free to explore other options in life. Whereas my food rituals limited my ability to be involved in life, removing my ritualistic behavior opens up new vistas to be explored. I sometimes find an emptiness where food used to be yet I fill this void with positive self-statements and self-nurturing experiences.

*   *   *

Life is more complete when food is viewed in its proper perspective.

Learning new behaviors to replace old habits requires that I trust in my self-worth. I have faith in myself and affirm my ability to grow. I exercise my new attitudes daily and consider myself as someone who is new and special. I treat myself as I would a guest in my home. I tend to my needs and ask myself how I am feeling. Do I have what I want to make me content? Is there anything else that I could do for myself at this moment? I am my new self. I deserve attention and care. I continuously check with my body, particularly when my behavior and thought processes are new. Life's options begin with my affirming myself.

*　　*　　*

As I develop new habits and attitudes, I constantly check with myself about my comforts, as I would with a guest.

I am a part of the whole. I relate to others as my brothers and sisters. We have all been put on this earth for a special purpose. I am seeking to find the peace and unity within myself that would help me cooperate with others. I join others as a complete fulfilled person. I bring my strengths and weaknesses with me. I go beyond my struggles with food and other compulsions to relate to people. I am learning to relate from a point of health rather than from need or compulsion. I am open to changes in the relationships I have now as well as in new relationships. I look for paths in my life that lead me to self-satisfaction and meaningful relationships.

*   *   *

As I find peace and fulfillment within, I relate to others in meaningful ways.

Changing coping behaviors is allowing the unknown to become part of my everyday experience. Risk becomes that which provides me with opportunities for growth rather than something to avoid. There are days when it seems easier not to even try, not to set myself up for yet another possible failure and more comfortable to keep my eating patterns the same. I challenge the old belief system as I switch my focus to my body and its feelings and away from food. This technique takes sympathetic listening to the unmet needs and fears that accompany growth and risk — reaching out to the unfamiliar, with which there is no guarantee. I employ the positive coping skills of relaxing, asking for support, distracting myself with a healthy new pattern and becoming assertive and challenging my skills.

*   *   *

Today I choose not to rely on my former coping skills but to support my own growth.

When confronted with an uncontrollable urge to eat, I now automatically switch my attention to my body to discover where I experience this feeling. I imagine a light travelling through my body, illuminating my feelings. I am then able to get in touch with these body feelings which may translate into past memories or a new discovery about my emotional reason to eat. The light leads the way for my discovery of myself. As I come upon the reason for my compulsion, life suddenly appears hopeful. I have the freedom to choose whether I wish to continue eating or whether I wish to experience and express my feelings without the hindrance of food.

* * *

I am able to see my compulsions illumined in the light of self-discovery as I understand and express my feelings.

I awake today with a sense of adventure. I approach my recovery from compulsive eating as a journey into my inner core, my true self. My life has somehow led me to this point in my recovery. I am now going to take a leap and get to the central issues involved in my compulsive eating. I am aware that although my environment has been an influence in my compulsive eating patterns, I am the only one who can truly help myself recover. I am responsible only for myself and my actions. I enjoy the feeling of freedom that comes with choice. Choosing to eat in response to physiological hunger frees me from eating or restricting food in response to emotions. I go with the flow of my internal cues as I express my feelings.

* * *

I embrace this opportunity for independence.

My goal for recovery is to resolve the past so that I may live in the present and direct my energy to solving my life's problems without relying on the old maladaptive family patterns. When I find myself in an uphill struggle with my eating disorder, I ask myself what am I resisting? What is still holding me back? What am I unwilling to release? I am aware that the hold of the past is a powerful force in life and yet I am ready to move into new territories to establish my own history. I realize that if I make any mistake in my life now, I want that mistake to be of my own choosing rather than a holdover from the past. I am in charge of my own destiny by the choices I make today.

*   *   *

Freedom to me means weaving into my new tapestry of life today that which I choose from my life in the past.

Today I look at all the "shoulds" in my life. When I listen to all the things I *should* do, I am dealing with preconceived notions about life in general. I am asking myself to look at a possible static existence around rules for eating, living and relating to others. I actively question each issue on my list of "shoulds" to see if they are life-promoting or life-stifling. I judge this by my reaction to each item on my list. For each "should," I think of an alternative activity and imagine myself being engaged in it. I compare the two activities and listen with my body as I read each alternative. I know by my response which item is life-promoting and which is life-restricting. I give myself permission to begin to live with the alternative that feels right for today and encourage myself to stay alive and open to change even with the new solutions.

*   *   *

My challenge is to live on a moment-by-moment basis.

I shift my focus to living and participating fully in the present. It encourages me to express my thoughts and feelings in the moment. I no longer concentrate on the past or the future. Living in the moment is a great challenge for me. Fears, worries and lack of trust in others kept me locked into the past. As I focus on the moment at hand, I am able to conquer my regrets of the past and fears for the future and to release the need to plan each and every moment. As I release the hold the past has had over me, I am able to create a life that is fulfilling.

* * *

I am fulfilled in the present as I give myself everything I need right now.

I inspire myself and so I am a motivator to others. I set my own standards of behavior. I consider others in my life — but from a point of self-possession. When I have gained my own approval for my actions, then I am able to release the expectations others have about me. This increases my responsibility because my actions are directed by me and for me rather than for others. As I choose to act only on my own behalf, I reap the rewards of stability. I am aware that the results of my actions *will* create changes in others around me. But I am willing to take this risk as I know that the end results will be positive.

* * *

I affirm my intentions for my life as I act responsibly.

Peace of mind and success come from knowing that the risks and changes I face during my recovery are made with my belief in myself and my self-worth. I act in my best interest in each change I make. I consider others in my life when I make decisions which affect them, yet I no longer give myself away. I now know that food was a part of that pattern. I reduce my emotional need for eating in each situation in which I formerly used food to soothe myself. I am putting myself before the problem rather than allowing the situation to control me. I am willing to work with others when negotiation and compromise are needed. There is power and freedom in my new way of seeing myself.

*   *   *

I release my need to care for everyone and lose myself.

Binges begin and end with unexpressed anger. When my day does not go right or someone makes some thoughtless remark or I choose not to assert myself or I recall memories of being used or victimized, I binge. I address this coping mechanism today as I acknowledge its lack of effectiveness. First, I actively work on reducing the number of binges by stopping myself for at least five minutes and listening to my body to see how I am feeling at this particular moment. Then I give myself permission to eat as I look to other ways to rid myself of my anger. I may begin by writing, talking with someone, moving my body gently to music or just relaxing as I focus my mind *away* from food and onto my feelings. I encourage expression of my feelings and seek the support I need to have these feelings validated.

*   *   *

I allow myself to choose in the moment in my best interest.

286

I release my feelings of pride and embrace true humility. I acknowledge the mistakes of the past as I make reparations today. I prepare for tomorrow by accessing my feelings about my past so that I may let them go. Carrying around the weight of the past is evident in my posture, musculature and the way I hold my body. My body deserves to be free. I develop some physical and mental ritual that encourages and symbolizes my transformation in this area. I freely release the past and my guilt and remorse as I make changes for the future. I change my relationship to my body as I step forward into the present. The body-mind connection is strong. I notice a shift in where I hold the weight in my body. I am living proof of my ability to take my life into my own hands.

* * *

I prepare for tomorrow as I make amends for the past and release my ego, shame and guilt.

287

On days when I am physically tired or emotionally exhausted, I pay special attention to my propensity to slip into previous eating patterns. I call on my new patterns to replace any desire to eat for emotional reasons. On the other hand, I make sure that I am eating to recharge myself physically. Balance is called for in times of stress. I begin to effect this balance on a physical level, knowing that emotional stress takes time to overcome. I soothe myself physically with baths, walks, asking to be held or whatever calms me. I approach each situation with a new set of tools that I have acquired in the process of recovery. I am true to myself and my process of recovery.

*　　　*　　　*

I establish my own boundaries as I image myself so that I may retain my sense of integrity.

Restricting my diet sets me up to crave for more of the foods I deprive myself of. Dieting puts stress on my body, my relationship with others, my productivity and my ability to concentrate on the task at hand. Dieting increases my obsession with food. I am learning not to diet but to listen to my body's needs. At first, this method may be risky for me. Yet as I improve my skill in listening to my body, I find the natural progression of experiencing hunger and responding to it immensely satisfying. Along with eating, I am allowing my feelings to surface and I express them in the moment. I discover that no one loses love for me by my expressing my feelings. On the contrary, people respect me and my new-found assertiveness.

*   *   *

As I respect my body's needs, it is easier for me to respect and honor my emotional needs as well.

Sometimes I feel that my life is a lie. I show the world the person I have strived to be for others — the performer, the helper, the savior, the strong one. What I show is what others have always wanted me to be for their own needs and for my need to please them and be accepted. I now risk exposing my inner child. On the inside, I have all of these feelings of isolation and vulnerability that I am afraid to show the outside world. I now realize that my sensitive, instinctual side is the child whose feelings have been ignored for many, many years. I am now learning to befriend and nurture that child so that the child can begin to feel strong and safe. I am teaching the child about feelings as I learn the nature of my needs. I am allowing the child free expression.

*　　*　　*

I remind myself that I am never too old or too late to connect with my inner child.

Cultural expectations of a man's or woman's shape no longer influence my goals for myself. It is freeing to be released from the group norm. I no longer rely on or hope for a certain body size or shape for my sense of importance. My body is acceptable the way it is today. My body is lovely. If I choose to set standards for myself for a short-term goal, I set a healthy realistic standard. My weight is no longer the central focus of my existence. I choose to emphasize other positive aspects of myself. I love and approve of the shape of my body. I enjoy my body when I express my sexuality in a positive healthy manner.

*   *   *

Today I release myself from the influences of established norms and ideas and courageously set my own standards of acceptance.

Today I make a list of the healthy options I have to soothe myself. What are my diversions other than food for celebrating happy occasions? I begin discarding the old belief system that has been in place with regard to food and emotions and replace it with powerful new beliefs. The new belief system focuses on the here-and-now as if I am making these decisions about feelings and expression for the first time. The past does not influence my decisions for today. I am able to resist the strong pull of the past by focusing on my goals of recovery. I forgive myself for actions in the past, knowing that I wish to move on in life. I choose new ways of relating to myself and others.

*   *   *

I free myself from the burden of the past as my beliefs change to accommodate my growth.

My environment is calming for me when I choose to have my meals. I remove distractions so that my body and mind may relax. Breathing deeply, I turn my attention to my body. I evoke peaceful images in my mind as I gradually establish my body in the here-and-now. I enjoy food which satisfies my body. I select my meals from foods I really want to eat. I appreciate my choices and enjoy the way my body gives me messages about what I wish to eat. I respect my body's cues when it signals fullness. I eat only to the point of satisfaction and I relax and allow my body to digest the food. Meals are a pleasure now as I am in touch with my body.

* * *

I am relaxed in body and mind as I establish contact with my body and enjoy the foods I want to eat.

There are days when I wish to celebrate my meals by setting a pleasing table and treating myself to the experience. I stay in the moment as I enjoy my food. I keep my eating at a comfortable pace while I savor the taste of the food. Because I am alive and present in my body, I release my fear of having a voracious appetite. My appetite is appropriate for my natural body size. As I change my eating patterns, my desire for food will vary from day to day in conjunction with physical activity. I set limits for the amount of food I eat by deciding on my level of physical comfort. I stop when I feel satiated.

*   *   *

I remove the habit of eating too much by concentrating on my body and staying in the moment.

Facing my struggle with food further involves me in addressing the issues behind food. I no longer use my body and my weight as a scapegoat. I feel stronger each day as I restructure my way of thinking. I am accountable for my behavior. As I use the information I am gathering about myself and my relationships with others, I am more free to express my true feelings. My protective cover of food and weight have been lifted and I face the rest of my life with a joy I have never allowed myself to feel before. My feelings lie deep within me. I access the emotions gradually, which gives me time to assimilate them. I avidly pursue my goal of being comfortable with my body and my weight.

*   *   *

The cornerstone of my self-worth lies in my acceptance of my body image.

Looking back at my life, I acknowledge that I have had successes despite my struggle with food. I am pleased not to have to hide behind the issue of weight and shape to fully acknowledge myself today. The problems with food are slowly but surely changing in intensity and frequency as I make plans for other important goals in my life. I am capable of continuing to succeed in life as I fully strive to grow. Releasing my compulsion with food and weight leaves me much time and energy to be even more positive and successful. I nourish myself emotionally with a positive recounting of my past. I trust myself to forge ahead with more success which reinforces my sense of self-worth.

*   *   *

I base the hope for my future success on past accomplishments.

As I nurture myself, I fully accept my natural body type. Nature has endowed me with unique physical characteristics which enhance my self-esteem. As I look at my body in the mirror, I deliberately focus first on the whole body and notice my proportions and how it all fits together. Then I focus on my particular strengths and openly praise myself. As I look at areas of my body with childhood hang-ups, I begin saying gently to each part that I accept it as an aspect of my lovely body. I accept my body's strengths and weaknesses as part of the whole. If I choose to separate one or more aspects of my body, I make a pact with myself today to focus only on the positive points. I think of my body positively.

*   *   *

I release my defensive hold over my body and allow the soft flow of acceptance to ease into my body-mind interaction.

My inner voice has become my friend, my encouragement to take one more step on the path toward self-enrichment. I am continually motivated by my powerful self-love. I am able to acknowledge that love has much more dynamic power than self-loathing. Self-love means going with the flow of life in the moment. Self-loathing held me back from life and risks, which is in direct opposition to the natural order of life. Self-love has more energy since there are no conflicts or obstacles in its path. Loving is self-generating and life-promoting. Self-love produces commitment to myself and to others that reinforces my positive focus in life.

*   *   *

The positive charge of love's energy takes me forward in growth and frees me of any restraints in my life.

The most important evaluation about myself and my recovery is my self-evaluation. I anticipate my continued growth and success each and every day now that I am in charge of my emotional, physical and spiritual life. As I review each day, I focus on the positive but realistically evaluate any stumbling blocks in my path. I recognize my accomplishments and my contributions to my success. I am my own personal coach. I encourage myself by providing guidance and praise. My inspiration comes from my ability to coach myself during positive times as well as during more stressful events. I tell myself the truth and allow myself to experience honest feelings. I give myself credit for genuine effort. I motivate myself each day with soothing, encouraging thoughts, assuring myself that the goal is attainable.

* * *

I provide support for myself as I approach life realistically.

When the ground is sliding from beneath my feet and the hope of overcoming compulsive eating seems far away, I put my faith in the Higher Power. I relax into the idea of having a purpose in life, even though in these moments a goal is illusive. I reach deep within myself to experience the true feelings. Panic and hopelessness are covering deeper feelings and possibly memories that I may be avoiding. I am comforted by the fact that food no longer hides this deep level of experience. I remember that I am never given more than I can handle. I encourage myself to allow the parental aspect of my personality to soothe the child within me. Accessing the child within gives me a more sympathetic understanding about my process. I am able to experience as well as witness the nurturing I need in this moment.

* * *

I handle the confusion of my compulsive behavior by going into the pain and focusing my attention on the present feeling.

Letting go of the past is essential for forgiveness. Everyone makes mistakes in life. Reliving those errors keeps me stuck in the experience of failure. Reviewing the past and the pain that accompanies it is necessary in the first stage of forgiving myself. Allowing the feelings to emerge is the next step. I experience these feelings as I process the past. Visualizing myself moving into the light of a new phase allows me to focus my energy on the present and to move away from expending energy on the past. I am able to experience the present with a lightness of heart as I accept my humanity. Perfectionism is a dilemma of the past. Forgiveness and inner peace are possible for me today and always.

*   *   *

Each day becomes a new experience for me as I review and let go of the past, moving into the light of forgiveness.

I am confident about all of my affairs in life. I relate well to others and handle myself with ease and grace. I am the living vision of my better self. My self-love and self-respect grow with each day. I am able to deal successfully with society's stereotypes as I have formulated my own personal style. There is freedom in being my true self. Where before I was a conformist eager to fit in, now I set my own standards for my actions. I find that people are better able to relate to me as I am comfortable with and confident about myself. The more empowered I am by my sense of self, the more willing I am to risk reaching my peak potential. The sky is the limit for my personal achievement today!

*   *   *

I become more confident in my actions as I move beyond my compulsion to conform and set my own standards.

Assertiveness means being the initiator, being the active person in a relationship rather than reacting to another's initiative or move. Assertive behavior reduces the need to control others since I am in true command of myself. Being assertive reduces my anger or hostility in situations I previously perceived as being out of my control. I act in the moment and then I am able to let go of feelings about the situation, recognizing that many situations involve compromise. The difference between compromise and compliance is that I am actively negotiating rather than passively or angrily accepting each situation. Being assertive in each situation allows me to accept myself and my emotions as I am willing to share myself with others. This softens my approach and makes my negotiating more effective.

*   *   *

I initiate, assert, negotiate and compromise but never comply.

I appreciate my support system. It encourages me to reach for greater heights as I proceed through my recovery. I can see more clearly when others, who may have difficulties with their own recovery, might not be able to support me. When this happens, I am able to move on quickly without harboring resentments toward them. It is important that I be with people who have my best interest at heart. I know this by my bodily reaction to others when I reach out for support. When I am met and emotionally acknowledged, I feel uplifted and even exhilarated. My body feels warm and comfortable. The opposite is true if I am with someone who is not able to support me. I feel queasy and somewhat heavy as I return to a former level of functioning. My body is now the barometer of my emotional state. I honor my body's cues.

*   *   *

I seek the level of support I need to advance in recovery.

I optimize my substantial talent and abilities in all areas of my life and affirm myself each and every day. I integrate my thoughts and my feelings for optimum functioning. I am able to acknowledge my physical need for food as well as my emotional need for support and nurturing. The more care I give myself, the more love and energy I am able to give others. I enhance my concept of self from a position of having and giving love. The people in my life respond favorably to the renewed sense of self I derive from self-nurturing. I encourage others to do the same and at times help them in their own caretaking. This is the gift of life and my gift to life.

* * *

My ability to be responsive to my needs restores my internal energy system on even the most stressful of days.

I own my own feelings and express them
to others without blame or judgment. I no
longer abandon my feelings for the feelings
of another. I choose to express my emotions
and interact with others honestly. I experience the integrity that comes with honest
expression and in turn respect others as they
choose to express their emotions. I move
towards a future that has the spirit of vitality
and renewal as the essence of human interaction. As I interact on an emotional level, I am
aware of the necessity for my own boundaries to be flexible and yet protective of my
inner spirit. I appreciate myself as I commit
myself to loyalty and generosity in the development of my emotional expression.

*   *   *

*I can forgive myself and others for the past as
I am able to extend compassion from a point of
honesty.*

My motivation for recovery comes from within myself. I am working for better personal health, both physical and emotional. I am motivated to communicate with others openly as I continue in this process of recovery. I share my concerns, my needs and my fears. I express my humanity openly as I release the hard core of protection or the childlike neediness which may have been my style of relating. I perform for myself as I grow each and every day. I am vulnerable with others as I learn more about myself. I am open to transformation. I make an effort to resolve any conflicts that may come up each day so that I may focus my energy fully on recovery. I strive to be honest with myself and others, knowing that I am paving the way for the rest of my life. I am thankful for the opportunity for growth and change.

*   *   *

I communicate my humanity to others as I discard my need for protection and emerge in my vulnerability.

Coping with setbacks in my recovery is just as vital as affirming my successes. I acknowledge that the ebb and flow of life sets the pattern for any human endeavor. Each time I make a stride forward, I also may take a step backwards. I focus on the fact that the next time I gain a step, it will be from a position of greater strength and power. I further acknowledge that recovering from food issues differs from recovery from chemical dependency in that I do not give up the substance. The challenge of being faced with food each day serves to strengthen my commitment to recovery and the constancy allows me to be flexible.

* * *

I gamely accept setbacks in my recovery, knowing that every step backward strengthens the momentum of my progress.

I am my own best friend. I make a commitment not to abandon myself for the love and approval of another or to keep peace at the cost of myself. I can now acknowledge that I use food as a reaction to self-abandonment. I have, in the past, expected food to fill the void that I created when I gave myself away. Now I am no longer relying on food or dieting to validate my self-worth. I build my self-worth by affirming myself each and every day. I recognize the gains I have made. I enjoy the small things in life and my own company. I entertain myself with fulfilling tasks. I reach out for support when I choose and am able to accept the support I am offered. I feel complete within myself as I establish a sense of peace and balance in my life.

*   *   *

Today I seek only my own approval and will not desert myself for fear or favor.

I am victorious over my struggle with food. In becoming free of my obsession, I have learned that it was flexibility in my attitudes that was required for my success whereas I had always believed that control over my body and weight was the key. Flexibility has allowed me to go with the flow of my life and to eat when I experience hunger. I listen to my body for my choice of healthy food. My feelings, my body and my spirit are all working in unison. When I insisted on control, my focus was on external circumstances rather than internal. Relaxing my need for control has allowed me to shift my focus to my inner life which has quieted the voices of resistance. Once I have released the inner critic, I no longer have the desire to resist.

*   *   *

I go with the flow of life in the realization that fighting the current is often resisting change for the better.

In my interactions with others, I create all-win situations. I am as supportive of the success of others as I am of my own. In fact, I assess the level of my commitment to myself by my level of relatedness to others. I enjoy supporting myself as I enjoy supporting others. The energy I give to others reinforces my commitment to health and well-being on a universal level. Love has a way of coming back to me when I give it away freely. When I expect to be repaid for my gifts, I have not given of myself at all. The more I accept and love myself, the more I am able to love others. Love generates love. Positive energy breeds positive energy. I allow the positive energy around myself to flow into each aspect of my life, work and relationships. I am love in action as I care for myself and others.

* * *

My life is continuously being renewed by the love and energy I am willing to give others in supporting their endeavors.

The source of my strength is limitless. I call upon my inner strength in the face of opposition and oppression. I rely on my sense of values to support me in times of strife. I accept my values as my own as I am an example to others, yet I cannot expect to change another. I accept others because I can accept myself. I stand up for my beliefs because I am true to my values. I have unveiled a courageous nature as I release my compulsion with food. The effort I formerly put into food fostered my weaknesses. Now the energy I put into defining my sense of self in relation to the world encourages me to be strong as I courageously risk self-expression. My connection to the Higher Power is a never-ending source of strength I tap into. I support the inherent good in myself and others.

*　　*　　*

I represent emotional, physical and spiritual strength as I reinforce my values and beliefs.

Today I focus on the mind-body interaction. I accept the connection and embrace the opportunity to work from the inside out in making friends with my body. In visualizing my realistically best body, I encourage myself to reach for that goal. By setting limits on how I choose to live and by disciplining my desire to eat for emotional reasons, I accept responsibility for my choices in life. I keep the goal of my ideal, healthy weight in mind and have faith in my ability to achieve it. I visualize myself as confident and alive and truly owning my body. It is a gift from the Higher Power and I take care of my body with my mind by allowing myself to have the foods I choose to eat. Stopping when I am full is another way to respect myself and the signals which my brain gives my body. I trust my body now and look forward to a deepening relationship with myself.

*   *   *

I take care of my body, using my mind to make clear choices.

Freeing myself of the compulsion to eat is an uplifting experience. I accept that there are conflicting demands in me, one asking to eat anything and everything and another saying that the new way is working and is the road to health. When the old feelings come up, I know them and have identified their source dating to childhood or some other time of frustration or trauma. I accept that it was the only way I had to feed my anger or sense of isolation. I am able to let go of the darkness with the help and support of my friends but more important with the day-by-day help I have given myself. I reward myself for each small step in the direction of letting go of my compulsion with a treat not related to food. I practice acknowledging myself each day as my confidence and strength grow and my true self blossoms.

* * *

Each day I give myself something small, something that helps me to know my true worth.

I liberate myself from the prohibitions of my past. I discover the true pleasures of my body and the joy of feeling the true satisfaction of food again or perhaps for the first time. I plan my meals so that I can be assured of satisfying myself. That is the most important goal for me — self-satisfaction and contentment. As I release the conflict around food by giving myself the loving permission to honor myself and my desires, I am no longer concerned with being deprived. I allow myself the time to feel fullness so that I know when to stop eating. Getting to know my body in this way is very stimulating and exciting. I focus my attention, when I am not experiencing hunger, on something other than food. I have room for new ideas now since food has an appropriate place in my life.

*   *   *

I can release the struggle with food by giving myself permission to have what I choose.

In giving myself permission to eat, I accept my body's knowledge of its physical limits. I am able to satisfy my hunger as I assure myself of my body's ability to be satisfied. I trust that the spirit within me is radiating love and I trust in the manifestation of that love in my body as well as in my life. I go with the flow of life as I am confident and trusting in my faith in a power that is greater than I. When I am most vulnerable, I entrust my life in that power. I have trust in my abilities and as I go along life's way, I am learning to trust my physical limitations. I acknowledge my hope in my recovery as I acknowledge my faith in my body. Food is my body's nourishment just as hope and faith are my spiritual nourishment.

*   *   *

I reinforce my faith in my recovery as I trust my body's abilities and the Higher Power's help in overcoming its limitations.

The more sure of myself I become, the
more goals and direction I have. Just when I
reach a plateau, I find myself reaching for
greater heights. My spirit soars and my hope
for growth is replaced by fulfillment and
realization of yet another goal. Some of my
goals are small and some large, yet with each
accomplishment I feel continual growth and
the excitement of renewing my commitment
to myself. The more I grow and change, the
more of myself I become. I witness myself
blossom and notice the positive energy flowing both from me and towards me from
others who are also witnessing my growth. I
am an example to others who experience the
same conflict with food. My changing process is a continuous source of strength to
myself and others.

*   *   *

*Each success whets my appetite for further
goals and greater achievements, renewing my
commitment to growth and change.*

Moving into the light has a new meaning for me today. I am able to visualize myself getting closer to the goal of my normal healthy weight and am confident that the new me is possible. I support others in their search for self and interact with them in a more positive and direct way. I make my needs known as an adult would. I address the child within me and answer the needs I can fulfill. I am able to allow the child to play in a healthy way when appropriate and to channel my impulses when I know the timing is not to my benefit. I use positive words to comfort the child within and choose ways other than using food to nurture myself when I feel impulsive. I am aware that these feelings will continue to come up in my life. I am confident now that I can handle them in a way that leaves me feeling centered in my body. I honor the light of life within me.

* * *

As the inner light shines through me, I visualize the new me.

I am open to receiving messages from my intuitive process that is working for me at all times. I am able to acknowledge that in the past I have blocked out the subtle signals my mind and body were giving to me with the cycle of control or loss of control over food. I learned this as a needy child. Now moving into adulthood, I am aware that that method is out of the scope of my healthy choices. I know that the maturation process begins when I am able to release my dependency needs. Letting go of my dependency with food is my major accomplishment. I notice that I now adopt healthy, interdependent relationships with people. I know that my relationships are changing by the people I choose. My instincts are becoming stronger as I acknowledge them daily.

*   *   *

As I respect my inner signals, I am rewarded by their continual support and reassured by my response.

319

I remove the scales as the barometer of my self-esteem. I focus on attributes that make up my core self to develop a positive image of myself. I assess my physical characteristics on the basis of function and health prior to judging myself. I also remove societal pressures to conform to an ideal of beauty that is not possible for me without maintaining an eating disorder. As I become more open to accepting myself on an emotional level as well as a physical level, I find that I am less focused on weight and more focused on the strengths of my personality. My ability to initiate new measures of self-assurance is enhanced as I release weight as a measure of acceptance.

*   *   *

I manifest to the world my real self as I develop self-assurance.

320

I open my heart to the small voice within me that consistently urges me on towards health and well-being. I see this voice as being my connection to the Higher Power and the source of my indomitable will. In order to stay connected to this inner voice, I have to pay attention to my connection to the universe, to my environment and to other people in my world. I also have to pay attention to myself and to the signs that I am truly committed to continuing on this path of growth. I know my actions are right for me when my thoughts, beliefs and actions are congruous. It seems that deprivation of food or compulsive eating interrupts the natural flow of the body as part of the universe. I am a part of the universe. I find myself choosing more natural foods to satisfy my body and my attitude towards healthy functioning.

*   *   *

I am a part of something bigger than myself and my participation in the universe is in keeping with the plans of the Higher Power.

When I focus my attention on recovering, I know I must go beyond my conscious belief about the body I have been given in this life and focus on the inner life which corresponds with a greater pulsating life. I follow my instincts and know when I connect with the Higher Power. My physical form and my attitudes, values and beliefs around this form have kept me locked into a way of life that no longer works for me. True change comes from within, from allowing myself to live, to participate in life and to gradually learn to accept myself with all of my strengths and weaknesses. I am aware now that it is a choice. While the past cannot be reconstructed, today and tomorrow can be different. I believe that I have all I need now to begin this process of change.

*   *   *

I understand now that if I allow my focus to be on physical reality only, I will remain trapped in the past.

My desire to create balance in my life stems from a deep longing for continuity and peace. I focus on my inner processes as I strive to maintain harmony in my life. I begin with myself when I wish to achieve any change rather than focusing on others. I look to the results of my interactions to match my internal expectations of balance and harmony. I move from a position of inner strength which is reflected in my movements as well as in my behavior and attitudes. I feel the freedom to be myself in all interactions as I support my personal expression. I experience the validation of my feelings as my inner and outer life are synchronous with each other.

*   *   *

I remove the self-deprecating thoughts and patterns of behavior that served to keep me out of balance with myself and others.

Each day I awaken to a new commitment to honor myself as my growth process unfolds. I am committed to allowing myself the room to grow just as I would a child of mine. Experiencing my inner self on the basis of love and acceptance is an opening that frees me to integrate my new awareness from the point of view of freshness and joy. I am accepting myself as my true concern for my growth is evident in my actions and thoughts. I encourage myself to explore new options, try new foods, wear new and exciting colors which reflect my growth and to make friends with those I admire. What I see in them is also a part of myself. I am worthy of my newfound love and attention. I honor my natural attraction to life and health.

*   *   *

I give myself room to grow when I accept myself as worthy of all the love and attention I am attracting.

My feelings and thoughts about my body improve each and every day. I notice the positive aspects of my body rather than look for weaknesses. I have discarded the need to continuously reaffirm myself in the mirror as well as check my weight on a scale. I have developed more realistic standards for myself with regard to internal and external characteristics. I strive to be my best self without the pressure to perform for others. My own standards are made by me for myself. My self-worth is based on a realistic appraisal of what I want for myself. I utilize my gifts to the best of my ability.

*   *   *

I find that as I am more comfortable with my body, I am more involved in life.

I have a healthy, realistic body image. My positive sense of self is further enhanced by my positive body image. I continue to break through barriers as I choose to limit myself less and less. Each day I notice the strength of my body as I consciously appreciate it for sustaining itself through my bout with compulsive eating. I willingly confront preconceived notions about my concept of self and my body image. I challenge the limits of my inner strength as I learn to accept myself as I am. I know that I am not able to change what I do not accept. I appreciate my body as it is, prior to initiating any change. I quiet the critical voice in me as I love my body unconditionally. Besides its physical beauty, I also affirm my body's miraculous functioning.

*   *   *

I am open to keeping my body as it is since I acknowledge my positive characteristics.

I focus on the positive events in my life. I count my blessings and am thankful for them. I experience the goodness of my friends' love and caring. The joy of life filters in through everyday events. I am loved and I feel the presence of the Higher Power working within me. As I reach out to others, I touch their inner spirit. I am able to see the real self in each person and experience the inner goodness. This frees me from becoming unnecessarily involved in aspects of others' lives that do not concern me. I choose the level of my involvement with others as I actively direct my own life. I am available to myself as I am available to my friends and loved ones in their times of need. I trust in the natural order of life and the natural give-and-take in my interactions with others.

* * *

I reach out to others with love and acceptance, for the inner self I see in them is also a part of myself.

Generosity comes from a place of completeness and wholeness within me. When I feel that I have taken care of myself, I am more able to give from a place of true caring. When I get my needs met, I am freer to interact and be present in the moment. Having food take on the primary importance of fulfilling a physical need removes it from being an obsession to fill an emotional need. I am the mother to my growth process. I release the old way of relating to food. If I am emotionally involved with some idea, person or event, I caution myself against comfort eating. I am generous in taking care of my emotional needs before I reach out to food. Life holds for me the magic and wonder of a child as I look to more fruitful, benevolent ways of comforting and rewarding myself in times of need.

*   *   *

I begin today to respond to myself as a mother would to an infant.

As I place my faith in the Higher Power, I feel a sense of renewed strength in the process of growth and in my relation to food. I release the stringent control over my diet. I reflect on the abundance of food around me, knowing that there will always be enough food for me and my family to eat. It is a feeling of deprivation that sets me up for binge/restrict cycles. Eating much more than enough at each meal is a signal that I am still fearful of not getting some basic need met in my life. If food is associated with positive forces in my life, I can affirm my positive association and remind myself that these forces are present in the healthy care of my body. If food is associated with deprivation in my life, I can remind myself of my new attitude towards giving to myself to satisfy my body.

*   *   *

I choose to keep only those attitudes that are healthy for me.

My faith in myself and my belief in the Higher Power is a private affair. I choose to nurture this power I have incorporated in myself as my attitudes and actions manifest the strong sense of self. I have the capacity to give to myself and others, the desire to befriend others who are in need and the ability to rely on my faith in my self-worth to carry me through life's journey. This strength and sense of survival is the healthy aspect of my personality. I look at my inner strength and compare it to a bank account. If I deplete the resources, I have nothing for myself or others. If I spend reasonable amounts, I have the original amount plus the interest. Giving my source of strength away means starting from the bottom, from emotional depletion each time I tap my inner spirit. This spirit is gentle as well as strong. Both aspects require care and protection if I am to remain effective in this world.

*   *   *

I choose to focus on my strength as a gift which I have the responsibility to nurture.

I am able to conquer my old belief system as I fervently express my new attitudes about my weight and my body. My weight is simply a measure; it is not a statement about my value as a human being. My strength of character comes from within and radiates outward. I have the time and energy to nurture my true gifts as I become less and less preoccupied with food and weight. I am amazed at the energy that is available to me as I release my obsession. Developing the strong aspects of my character is reinforcing, whereas spending time and energy on food is ultimately draining. There are boundless rewards in developing my gifts while the rewards are fleeting in directing my energy towards food.

*   *   *

As I conquer false beliefs and find the energy to nurture my true gifts, I find greater goals to motivate myself.

I am able to release unhealthy defenses as my sense of self grows stronger. I am more aware of myself as a productive, spontaneous person as I affirm my positive traits daily. I demonstrate a spirit of openness and trust as I am willing to be seen by others. Emotional comfort is offered to me by others as I am free to express my vulnerability in a healthy way. I exhibit the courage of self-expression as I am willing to risk exploring the priorities in my life. I move towards the spirit of wholeness in my growth as I forgive myself and release the past. My foundation for future growth becomes stronger as my sense of self is enriched by my life-experience.

*   *   *

As I drop my defenses and freely express my vulnerability, I gain emotional riches hitherto unknown.

332

I lost touch with my body when hunger ceased to have meaning for me. Ignoring my body cues has become a habit in every aspect of my life. I reaffirm my commitment to myself as I learn to listen to my body. I respect my body's signals as I progressively refine my natural instincts. I further my goals by reflecting accurately in my behavior what I am feeling on the inside. I honor my feelings through honest emotional expression. My behavior is no longer based on what I think is expected of me by others. It is a true, spontaneous expression of my internal emotional life. I create my own sense of continuity and security.

*   *   *

The consistency in my feelings and expressions have become a safe haven in a seemingly unpredictable world.

I reach deep within myself to find the answer to my quest for true meaning in my life. I go beyond my apparent struggle with food to reach my goal of peace within. I look to the Creator's intuitive aspect in my thoughts and actions to stimulate new attitudes and beliefs. The expression of my Creator's intuitive thinking is represented by a lack of restriction or restraint in my behavior. I am able to release unwanted habits, unnecessary weight and nonsupportive people in my life as I explore my true sense of values that will reflect the integrity of my inner life. My body, my feelings and my spirit all work in unison to promote the emergence of my better self.

* * *

I have become aware that my true strength lies within me in my spirit.

My awareness of the truth about myself and my life is comforting to me now. Just as I had made a habit of running away from myself in the past, I now make it a daily practice to acknowledge something about my life, both past and present. I allow myself to focus on the past only when it serves to help my life be more complete in the present and in the future. I am now completing the process. I remember the event which led me to this place of discovery. I know that my life now and in the future is based on my new belief system and on my confidence in myself and my abilities. I am continuously reinforced by my successes which, I notice, occur daily. Even small steps forward give me encouragement.

*   *   *

Breaking down the walls which helped me hide is reassuring for me.

I have previously nourished others to hide my own deep sense of emptiness. What I formerly considered selfless giving is no longer rewarding for me. I have given my own self away and wish now to reclaim it. I search deep within me to find what I like and appreciate about myself. I write them down and keep the list handy during this day to reaffirm my positive qualities. My goal for today is to focus on the qualities about myself which I truly enjoy and truly believe. Tomorrow I will repeat these qualities and add two attributes that I am striving to improve. I am my own cheering squad as I appreciate myself. I am beginning to check in with my own best friend — myself.

*   *   *

Today I disabuse myself of my mistaken sense of giving and reclaim my true self by paying attention to my positive qualities.

I accept my fundamental need to grow and fulfill myself in this life. I accept the competency, the achievements and the choices which make up the rich tapestry of my life. I accept the qualities which continue to require reinforcement from me in order to blossom. I see myself as I am now and I see myself in the future as I focus on my goals. When I think of my ideal self, I focus on a realistic goal both in terms of weight and body size and in terms of personal and professional development. I am my positive self-statements. I am a realist. I strive to be my best and accomplish what I am able to accomplish. My demands on myself are also realistic, leaving time for play and reflection, knowing that the true artist takes time to refurbish the self. I am the creator of my own life.

* * *

As I create anew the rich tapestry of my life, I see myself with the eyes of an artist rather than with the eyes of a critic or judge.

Asserting myself makes me accept the power that is rightfully mine. My affirmations help me in knowing myself and taking an assertive stance on my rights and privileges. I notice that as I respect myself, others also respect me. Whereas I used to wait for another's acknowledgment of my value, I now discover daily that my own inner sense of self and my inherent worth serve to bolster my self-esteem and command respect from others. My growth takes place from the inside. Now is the time to devote my nurturing energies towards myself. I also notice that my posture reflects my sense of self. As my posture and my words match, I am more effective. I work on integrating the two because I now know the feelings and the rewards it brings. I am attuned to my body's signals as I am present and spontaneous in my self-expression. My body and mind function as one.

* * *

I make eloquent statements about myself as my physical and verbal expressions match.

I now look forward to my meals each day. I know that the size of my appetite is adequate to sustain me and to fill me on a physical level. I am able to choose my food and be satisfied with what I have eaten. I can leave food on my plate if I am feeling full. This is a breakthrough for me! But, then, I am making progress in so many areas that I am getting used to breakthroughs. I am proud of the way I approach food. I am pleased that it is only one aspect of my life now. Food, though, is an important aspect of my life as it has taken its rightful place. I have grown past the need for food as comfort or solace. I foster open communication with others. My emotional and spiritual life have taken on greater significance as I search for life's deeper meaning. The richness of my inner life nourishes my spirit.

*   *   *

I actively address my conflicts and search for resolutions within myself.

I am expanding my vision of my universe. I can see those who are really there for me and who are willing to support me in my search for my true self. These people are my true friends and their love and concern for me help me in accepting myself and taking in their love. At times, when I feel abandoned by others, I am actually abandoning myself. My friends may be supportive, but I am unable to see it at that particular time. It is vital for me at that time to be my own best friend. Only then can I truly accept the support of others and take in their love. This way I am able to break the patterns of co-dependency and have relationships that are interdependent, healthy and produce growth. The more I expect in loving myself, the more positive people I attract in my day-to-day life.

*   *   *

As I befriend myself and attract support from others, I see that it was I who had all along rejected myself.

The part of me that makes positive choices for my whole life is the healthy part. This part is spontaneous and living in the present but with one eye kept trained on the future. The child within me, who eats compulsively or restricts food to gain temporary control, makes decisions prompted by the neediness and immediacy of the desired results. I am patient with the child within me while recovery is taking place. I allow the child to express needs and make the decisions a child can make. I encourage the child to play and laugh. I accept the different parts of myself and know that the mature part had needs other than those the child can express. I am learning that my adult part needs mutuality and understanding in relationships and realistic goals that can help me in my development as a whole person — goals that can sustain me in the future.

*   *   *

I befriend all aspects of my personality and relinquish the need to control my self-expression.

Life is moving quickly these days. I am taking charge of my life and am able to feel the excitement of the possibilities for my future. I am amazed at the things I create when I am focused on my goal. Things seem to fall into place as if by design. I am now willing to accept the fact that I create my own life and opportunities. I accept my abilities and the positive, growth-producing atmosphere I create for myself. As I awake, I greet the day with joy and anticipation. I know that living this process of change on a daily basis keeps my hope of recovery alive. Life is much easier when I am ready to receive the challenges I am faced with. I know that I can accomplish whatever I choose to accept as my challenge.

*　　*　　*

What used to appear as overwhelming and frightening, now appears to me to be exciting and challenging.

Food has been a reward for me for most of my life. I can recall special people being pleased with me when I ate the food prepared for me. It was my way of being good to them at the same time I got my needs met. I am now trying to release my connection with food. It is possible for me to view food as a meal and as nutrition for my body. I eat no more to fill a space. I view my body as a temple and respect it. I no longer eat to please people or restrict food to resist people or remain in control. I am in control of my life. Even when I choose to comply with another's wishes, I am in control of my actions. I am in control even when I binge. I feel safe with food. Accepting my love affair with food helps me in making the desired changes in my life.

*   *   *

I can enjoy eating food without compulsion setting in or losing control.

It is my conviction that I am a worthwhile person. I look to past situations in my life to reinforce this belief and to the present moment to strengthen my belief in myself. Affirming this belief leads me to change my actions in relating to myself. I release my critical voices about my body and my actions. I release the conflicts that set up a vicious cycle of repeating the same actions. As I change my belief system about myself and my body, I agree to forgive myself for all the years I have been compulsive about food. I now choose to release the old belief system and to work out my problems in a positive, systematic way. Reviewing and changing negative thoughts help me to continually minimize the negative input in my daily life. Increasing the positive input insures my success in all areas of life.

*   *   *

I monitor my thoughts to spot any habitual negative thought pattern that may continue to creep into my awareness.

I am in the process of learning to trust my internal feelings — my natural reaction to people and events. I am filtering this through emotions of love for myself and others, without fear. I accept that my natural reaction is honest, but I do not always have to act according to it. In learning this, I am beginning to notice how my internal feelings are different from what I may say and do. I am learning to translate my internal feelings into external actions acceptable to me at this time. I am aware that I do not have to do this to the point of discomfort. Today I will make a note of one situation in which I can express myself so that my internal feeling matches my expression.

*   *   *

I am learning to translate my feelings into actions that are acceptable to me.

I am determined to focus my energies on my health. I notice the shift in attitude when I choose my food as a means to make myself healthy and strong. I use food as nurturance for my physical health and accept positive self-statements as nurturance for my emotional well-being. The two go hand in hand as I focus on the integration of a healthy attitude towards myself as a whole being. Food and the choice surrounding it are a part of the whole. I no longer focus on food as a separate issue as I focus on health in my recovery. I feel a shift towards wellness in my body as I experience the possibility to choose for my health. I will be able to recall the feeling and unite it with a positive thought in order to integrate the experience as I move towards wholeness.

*   *   *

As I reinforce my commitment to healthy changes, I automatically expand my level of awareness.

Following through with my commitments is my way of showing my level of involvement. I choose my commitments wisely and with discretion so that I may remain free to give. I enjoy the projects and the people I choose to involve myself with. I honor the gifts I have and thank the Higher Power for giving me the talents I can share with others. I enjoy the opportunities for manifesting my love by exploring my gifts in depth. When I thus nourish myself and my talents, I am refurbishing my inner strength. I am aware that giving to others can tap the source of this strength — my inner spirit. I know through experience that I can give to others only what I am able to give to myself. My commitment to others is stronger when I reinforce on a regular basis my commitment to nourishing myself.

*   *   *

Renewing my commitment to myself refurbishes my talents so that I may involve myself more with others.

347

As each day dawns, I renew my commitment to my personal growth. I free myself from the past as I am able to release grievances from my day-to-day life. I acknowledge my past and have nurtured myself through the grieving process. I am free from my past as I make choices based on my best interest. I learn how to support further growth by encouraging myself to try new experiences. I judge my success based on how I feel with each new accomplishment. I no longer look outside of myself for a measure of my success. Success is now translated as a positive sense of self, a positive feeling of self-worth. I am familiar with the feeling of positive self-esteem as I become my own best friend.

*   *   *

As I wake with the dawn of each new day, I feel renewed by my self-parenting.

I live up to my own standards for myself. I thank my Higher Power for the opportunities that life has presented to me for my own growth. My recovery is possible because of the people who have come into my life and my growing ability to avail myself of life's opportunities. Each time I revisit my compulsive behavior around food, I do so with a new awareness of the cause of this particular episode. I choose to see each relapse as a single, unconnected event which can be overcome. I encourage myself to continue to look at my behavior without judging my self-worth on episodic eating patterns. I am a powerful human being with resources to overcome any struggle in life. Each step forward is a positive new memory upon which I base my hope for today and tomorrow and tomorrow.

*   *   *

As I reflect on each day, I am aware that each situation is new and my reactions are to that particular situation.

Opportunities for success lie before me. I choose the path of hope and success and possibilities that will enhance my experience of life. I am the dynamic force in my life. I look at my skills and continue to build on my strengths. My strength comes from knowledge of myself, knowing my behavior and thoughts, and from my awareness of my feelings. I listen to others as I reinforce my faith in myself. My sense of self comes from my truly valuing myself. My contribution to the world is based on my ability to first affirm myself. I can offer to others only that which I have learned about myself. I am the dynamic growth force in my life.

*   *   *

I enjoy my success as an aspect of personal fulfillment rather than as my reason for gaining in self-worth.

Living in the present releases me from preconceived notions. I put my faith in the Higher Power to direct me into the future as I live my life in the here-and-now. Each moment is enriched by my faith in the Higher Power. I am grateful for today. When I take the time to experience the present, I appreciate the beauty of each moment as I feel life blossom within me. I go beyond my expectations of yesterday when I remove the past as a reference for today. Being truly open to the experience of the present means having a willingness to explore new alternatives to old problems. I can remove emotional eating from my life, knowing that it had a purpose. My growth at many levels has made it unnecessary and unsatisfying. New adaptations are required for the new levels of my growing awareness. I am choosing more natural, rhythmic responses to life.

*   *   *

I find that I can accomplish more on a day-by-day basis with a focus on the present.

I embrace this time of growth in my life as a time of strengthening my personal power. I have formerly reacted to situations and have been strengthened by my ability to survive. I am more than a mere survivor as I take charge of the conditions in my life. I release the patterns of the past that made me a reactive participant rather than an active innovator. I now act in my best interests. I complete the circle of the past by taking charge of my life. My eating patterns are a part of the past. It was my way of reacting to unpleasant surroundings and conditions in my life at that time. Taking charge of my life also means taking charge of my body. I choose to eat foods that are pleasing to me, to eat when I experience the signals of hunger and to stop eating when I am full. I am mobilizing all of my energy to promote life-enhancing patterns.

*   *   *

I am at the forefront of all negotiations that affect my day-to-day existence.

352

As I look around, I see the wonder in the eyes of the children in all of us who are encouraged to live life to the fullest. Living and loving is the essence of life. Rather than searching for the problems of human nature, I choose to focus on its beauty and wonder. I first see the ability to survive. After the survival needs are met, I see the joy of truly living. I acknowledge that food and warmth are the first requirements for survival. Food can mean many things to us — love, joy, comfort, camaraderie and a guarantee that we will survive. As I grow emotionally and assure myself of the value of self-love, I begin to trust others and allow myself to live. Gradually, I am able to give up my dependence on food as I establish trust in myself, my body and my self-efficacy. Life begins anew today.

* * *

Today I look at living from the perspective of beauty and joy.

My body is a sympathetic extension of my internal emotional life. I think positive, health-producing thoughts about my body. Positive thoughts and attitudes help create positive feelings about my body's image. The boundaries I establish through my movements and my attitudes are a direct expression of the state of my feelings. I express my feelings nonverbally through my body image and my movements. I reinforce the positive changes in myself with a new respect for my body. I enhance these changes with an outward expression either in dress or through other personal messages to myself. Each time I witness the signal of change, I stop to reaffirm my commitment to growth and fulfillment.

*   *   *

My body's image, movements and expression are outward extensions of the positive changes taking place within.

I am learning to soothe myself without food. I direct my attention to the problem at hand, knowing that food is no longer an effective way of handling my anxiety. I break each situation down into smaller parts in order to focus on the crux of the matter. In response to physiological hunger, I nourish myself with food. I may eat many times during the day, which helps me to calm myself physically. Only after I have trained myself to eat when hungry can I separate the issues of frustration and anxiety from food. I am prepared to address any issues that may arise in life. I am more available to the people in my life since I no longer rely on food or fasting to resolve my problems. I can accept the pleasures and pain of life. I accept my power and own my natural ability to handle life.

*   *   *

The more secure and nourished I feel, the more I can solve life's daily problems with my mind rather than by eating my troubles away.

355

I am learning to think positively about myself, my body and food. I am aware of it when negative thoughts come into my mind. Each time I recognize a negative thought, I make an effort to stop thinking the thought and deliberately turn it into an affirming self-statement. I am aware that negative thoughts produce negative results and positive thoughts are the road to self-acceptance. Negative thought patterns keep me locked into the need to eat. Positive, affirmative thoughts allow me to choose the path I will take. Positive thoughts are open-ended. I replace negative thoughts with an open-minded attitude — one that is tolerant and conducive to change.

*   *   *

I challenge negative thoughts as if I were defending a child or my best friend.

I am compassionate and realistic in my expectations of myself. I look at myself each and every day as I strive for a better understanding of what my goals are for the day. I am aware that my attitudes towards food and eating change gradually. I accept my relationship with food as it is today. I can only change what I am able to accept. If I continue to binge or restrict food, I strive to accept each incident as a single event rather than as an accumulation of past events. I can let go of my litany of criticisms as I acknowledge my position in this process of change. I accept that I have been my worst enemy and that now I am becoming my own best friend. I am supportive of myself in the present moment. I am at peace with myself as the mechanics of acceptance are at work in my life.

* * *

I move from negativity to neutrality to acceptance.

I look at my body honestly and realistically without the judgments of the past. I accept my body as it is today. Each day I make an effort to compliment one more aspect of my body. I find that the more positively I relate to my body, the more I am able to satisfy my physiological need for food rather than my emotional need for it. I respect my body. I dress my body to call attention to the positive aspects of my physique. I listen to compliments and take them in as genuine statements of appreciation. My wardrobe reflects how I feel about my body in the present. I discard clothes that no longer fit me as I discover my true weight. I am able to wear any clothes I enjoy. I am pleased with my ability to choose clothes that are attractive. I live in the present. Self-acceptance paves the way towards freedom from the past.

* * *

My attitude towards my body is refreshingly new.

I am clear within myself about my commitment to change. My nonverbal behavior — my posture, my gestures and my facial expression — clearly communicate my personal feelings about my transformation. I believe in myself and my recovery. I am aware that this differs from dieting in that there is nothing concrete to follow, so I can never go off recovery. Backsliding is permissible and even expected in recovery. Each event of backsliding provides me with a new opportunity to learn about myself and my patterns. The ebb and flow of life gives me many opportunities to grow and change. I look at myself with an openness that encourages others also to be open with me. I am a catalyst for change. I promote love and self-acceptance each and every day.

*   *   *

Today as I feel myself relapsing into old behaviors, I assure myself that it is only a stage in letting go.

I focus my attention on the possibilities that are open to me. I consistently remind myself of the small successes I accomplish daily. I compliment myself on each small accomplishment. I know that the broader picture of change is a series of successes. My positive self-talk keeps my attention focused on the benefits of recovery. A journey is always begun with one step. I am committed to my changing self. I release any expectation of perfection as I travel along life's way. I embrace the goals that are attainable and release impossible expectations that previously kept me from changing. The evidence of my success is visible in every area of my life. I am careful to note those changes and praise my efforts. I choose health and well-being each and every day.

*   *   *

I realize that perfection is rooted in fear.

I am in charge of my beliefs and my behavior. I contribute to my continued success by allowing others to be responsible for their behavior just as I am responsible for my own. I enjoy being in charge of my life as I appreciate the openness I exhibit in daily situations. By not relying on preconceived notions of expected behavior, I open the door to the possibility of surprise and adventure. A small event may transform my life as I am open to change. I share myself and feel a communion with others. I value the contribution I make to the world. My personal power is reinforced by my positive self-talk as well as my openness. I contribute my strength to the world as I share my happiness with others.

*   *   *

I lay myself open today, without preconditions and expectations, so that growth and change may transform me.

My body is the temple of my inner spirit. I give my body the respect it deserves — not based on past experiences, actions or judgments but based on honoring the self unconditionally. I have respect for the essence of my true nature. I focus on the innocence of my spirit and give myself the credence that promotes growth. I judiciously choose what I put into my body to satisfy hunger as well as who I interact with on a personal and spiritual level. I choose to focus on the positive aspects of my physical self while learning to accept myself as I am today. I direct my attention away from future expectations as I focus on the present. I strengthen my attributes through positive affirmation and reduce the emphasis on perceived negative traits through thought-focusing.

*   *   *

I foster my own self-worth by honoring my spirit and accepting the natural guidance of my body.

I review my preconceived notions about the ideal body. I question where my ideas come from regarding my body and marvel at how little the perceived ideal corresponds to my best body. I actively work to change those ideals that may have come from ideas and bodies other than my own. I remove my attachment to ideals of the past as I allow my sense of my own body and the aesthetic appreciation of my body as it is today to evolve into a true validation of my positive qualities. I first work on accepting my body and then, once achieved, I focus on loving and honoring my body. I treat myself with the respect I have offered others in my life. I direct this feeling of unconditional acceptance and honor towards my whole self — spiritual, emotional and physical.

*   *   *

I gradually discard old beliefs about my body and uphold it to validate my positive qualities today.

I am free to express my feelings of self-love and desire for a healthy lifestyle. I am part of the whole that is moving towards the future filled with peace and contentment. I fulfill my potential in life as I begin to nurture my body, mind and spirit. I respond to others from a sense of aliveness and communion on the path of learning and growth. I am able to discern from a point of strength who in my life promotes this growth and who diminishes my capacity for fulfillment. I choose to be with those people who support my process of growth and who, in turn, I am lovingly able to support. As I act from my spiritual center, I notice that I am able to respond to my natural physical body and its honest needs.

*   *   *

I experience the true give-and-take of friendship and unconditional love and willingly participate in the natural flow of life.

I have the desire and the ability to see life clearly and realistically. I am trusting of and free to accept the challenge of living the life I have created for myself. I no longer live in the hope of having the perfect weight or body to complete my life. I am living with a firm conviction and belief in myself and choose not to abandon myself emotionally. No one can fix me, yet I trust that others in my life will support my honest efforts towards growth and personal fulfillment. My commitment to recovery from my eating disorder grows as my honest, loyal commitment to myself grows. I am emotionally secure in my love for myself and therefore I am able to meet others with true love and concern without a desire to possess or control them. I can take in the essence of others and accept them as they are.

*   *   *

I am in possession of myself as I become realistic about my life.

I open myself to the freedom of unconditional acceptance. I encourage myself to experience new or forbidden foods, to wear clothes that are becoming to me, to speak up when I have something to say and to risk being myself in each situation. I accept my natural body type and my weight at this moment. I choose not to live my life in the future ideal but to live it in the moment. I feel with my whole being — body, mind and spirit — the desire to overcome my eating disorder. It is in the experience of desire mixed with the beginnings of positive self-regard and deservedness that the miracle of healing and growth will happen. The beginning of this miracle starts with me and my willingness to examine and let go of old coping patterns that no longer bring results or pleasure to my life.

*   *   *

I accept myself unconditionally at this moment of becoming.

More Affirmation Books

DAILY AFFIRMATIONS: For Adult Children of Alcoholics
Rokelle Lerner

Affirmations are positive, powerful statements that will change the ways we think, feel and behave. *Daily Affirmations* has also been recorded on audiocassette, where author Lerner is joined by Dr. Joseph Cruse.

ISBN 0-932194-27-3 .... $ 6.95

Set of Six 90-Minute Tapes
ISBN 0-932194-49-4 .... $39.95

SAY YES TO LIFE: Daily Meditations for Recovery
Leo Booth

Say Yes To Life takes you through the year day by day looking for answers and sometimes discovering that there are none. Father Leo tells us, "For the recovering compulsive person God is too important to miss — may you find Him now."

ISBN 0-932194-46-X .... $ 6.95

TIME FOR JOY
Ruth Fishel

With delightful illustrations by Bonny Lowell, Ruth Fishel takes you gently through the year, affirming that wherever you are today is perfect and now is the *TIME FOR JOY!*

ISBN 0-932194-82-6 .... $6.95